Quia praeterii
Malitiori Ad Infinitum

Secretum tibi si au pvejst
Ad amicum abr...
Quod nec litt...
quoquam hom...
commi... ...m nec
TABELLION...

normele
domnul întuner
peste tot

THE ESSENTIAL
SUPERNATURAL™
ON THE ROAD WITH SAM AND DEAN WINCHESTER

THE ESSENTIAL
SUPERNATURAL™
ON THE ROAD WITH SAM AND DEAN WINCHESTER

NICHOLAS KNIGHT

FOREWORD BY ERIC KRIPKE

Additional material by Christopher Cerasi

Supernatural created by Eric Kripke

INSIGHT ◉ EDITIONS

San Rafael, California

INSIGHT
EDITIONS

PO Box 3088
San Rafael, CA 94912

FOR WEB EXCLUSIVE CONTENT!

f Find us on Facebook: www.facebook.com/InsightEditions

y Follow us on Twitter: @insighteditions

Library of Congress Cataloging-in-Publication Data available.

ISBN: 978-1-60887-145-2

Design by *tabula rasa* graphic design

ROOTS of PEACE   ● REPLANTED PAPER

Insight Editions, in association with Roots of Peace, will plant two trees
for each tree used in the manufacturing of this book. Roots of Peace is
an internationally renowned humanitarian organization dedicated to
eradicating land mines worldwide and converting war-torn lands into
productive farms and wildlife habitats. Together, we will plant two
million fruit and nut trees in Afghanistan and provide farmers there
with the skills and support necessary for sustainable land use.

Manufactured in China by Insight Editions

10 9 8 7 6 5 4 3 2 1

CONTENTS

FOREWORD

Look, I don't have to tell you: You get it.

If you've made the sizeable financial investment in this deluxe, all-class coffee-table book, then you're already a fan. Or maybe it's a few years from now, and you've purchased the book at steep discount. Either way, I appreciate the effort.

Still, my guess is, you're one of us. You get what we're making here—a whacked-out milk shake that's equal parts Sam Raimi, Peter Jackson, *Fletch*, *The Simpsons*, *Sandman*, *Hellblazer*, *Star Wars*, Joseph Campbell, hope, love, family, and AC/DC. Most people wouldn't dream of mixing such things. But you and I know—it's delicious. Irreverent, mythic, and just cool, pure and simple.

So here's a book that pays tribute to this weird little shared universe of ours. But more than that, it recognizes all the people who have worked so hard and sacrificed so much to bring it to life.

Like Jerry Wanek, the brilliant production designer who's defined the visual style of this show as much as anybody. And who's made a couple hundred wildly distinct motel rooms— no easy task.

Like Serge Ladouceur, the director of photography. You want to know the single hardest-working dude on the show? It's Serge. I've never seen him sit down or take a break, 15 hours a day, every day, as he creates our cinematic look, with a dignity and calm that I strive to emulate—but never do.

Like Phil Sgriccia, who's not only directed some of our very best episodes, but also oversees the editing of every one. Some of your favorites? The footage was crap. Phil tugged our butts out of the fire and made them work in the editing room.

Like Ben Edlund, the most talented writer I know. Yes, he pitches crazy stuff. But what people don't realize is how disciplined he is with structure and character. And how, behind the scenes, he's helped craft countless episodes. He makes all of us look better and smarter than we really are.

Like Sera Gamble, who makes these characters sound more human, and their dialogue more natural, than I ever could. She was handed this torch—and it's hot and painful to hold—and she's carried it to new places, illuminated new corners. I'm so, so proud of her.

Like Kim Manners, God rest his soul, who I still miss daily.

Like Jared and Jensen, who are the heart of all we do. We wouldn't have any of this without their talent and commitment. Some of the scripts are good; others suck out loud. But Jared and Jensen always make them emotional, real, and watchable. I love 'em like brothers.

Like Bob Singer, who literally taught me everything I know about this job and who has been my partner from the beginning. Bob is a humble guy and stays out of the spotlight. But the fact is, he's created this show every bit as much as I have. He deserves more credit.

Finally . . . like you. Yes, you. The fans. Because you're the reason *Supernatural* is on the air. You watch the episodes, buy the merch (like this book—thanks!), discuss online (and, yes, you drive me crazy, but I love you). Just like us, you live here. Like us, you've helped create this insane, symbiotic thing.

You're one of us. You get it. And for that, I thank you.

—Eric Kripke

OPPOSITE, TOP: Series creator Eric Kripke steps behind the camera to direct Kurt Fuller (Zachariah) in the season 4 finale, "Lucifer Rising." OPPOSITE, BOTTOM: Eric Kripke directs Jared Padalecki and Genevieve Cortese Padalecki (Ruby) in the final scene of "Lucifer Rising."

CHAPTER 1

SAM AND DEAN HIT THE ROAD

URBAN NIGHTMARES: CREATING *SUPERNATURAL*

Supernatural is a dream come true for me," declares creator Eric Kripke. The Ohio-born writer, director, and producer had been dreaming about creating a series of stories based on urban legends and American folklore since he was in the fifth grade. Throughout his career, first writing comedy movies, then writing and co–executive producing Warner Bros. Television's *Tarzan* TV series, he tried pitching his idea for a "gory, twisty series," but no studio was interested. Then his first horror script, *Boogeyman*, was produced, and suddenly he became known as a successful horror writer. Around the same time, *Lost* became a megahit that made every TV network want a twisty genre show. It was as if the Fates had intervened.

"I had a really good relationship with Warner Bros.," Kripke says. "They really appreciated how hard I worked on *Tarzan*, and I loved working with them. They said, 'What are you passionate about?' So I pitched them my [TV series] idea." Only, the pitch wasn't *Supernatural* as we now know it; it focused on a reporter who investigated urban legends. Warner Bros. still didn't bite, but they asked him if he had anything else. Fortunately, Kripke had an alternate approach prepared.

He pitched them the same idea, this time saying the TV show would revolve around two brothers cruising the country on a road trip. And this time Warner Bros. bit.

Interest from The WB, the TV branch of Warner Bros., soon followed. Kripke teamed up with executive producer McG (*Charlie's Angels*) and co–executive producer Peter Johnson (*Chuck*) at Wonderland Sound and Vision and together they brainstormed a pilot script that met the network's approval. Then director David Nutter came on board, and his extensive experience directing *The X-Files* and pilots for *Dark Angel*, *Roswell*, *Smallville*, and *Tarzan* gave The WB the confidence to green-light the show.

Kripke used the tagline "*Star Wars* and Truck Stop America" to shorthand the show. "Who wouldn't want to watch Han Solo and Luke Skywalker with chain saws in the trunk?" he asks rhetorically. The idea of having heroes who traveled Route 66 and "Truck Stop America" appealed to Kripke's personal sensibilities. "Small towns, blue-collar lifestyles, greasy diners, dive bars, beer, and cheeseburgers are the things I understand," he says, referring to his roots in Toledo, Ohio. But what's a

OPPOSITE: Jared Padalecki and Jensen Ackles share a laugh between takes during season 1. TOP LEFT: Jensen, Jared, and Misha Collins relax on the set of season 6's "The Third Man." TOP RIGHT: Jeffrey Dean Morgan, Jensen, and Jared rehearse a scene from season 1's "Dead Man's Blood." ABOVE LEFT: Jensen and Jared shoot a scene for season 6's "Like a Virgin." ABOVE RIGHT: Eric Kripke checks the setup of a scene between takes on location in Vancouver, British Columbia.

road trip without great tunes? To Kripke, that means classic rock blaring as loud as possible while speeding down two-lane roads that stretch into infinity. "There's something so mythic, so American, about that, and that's the energy I wanted the show to have." He was adamant that the show should have an "ass-kicking soundtrack."

Yet none of that would matter if they didn't find actors with the charisma of Harrison Ford and Mark Hamill. Especially since *Supernatural* only has two leads. Jensen Ackles read for the role of Sam Winchester first, but it quickly became clear that he suited the devil-may-care attitude of Dean perfectly. "Jensen's as charismatic [in real life] as he is on-screen," enthuses Kripke. Then in came Jared Padalecki, and he *was* Sam Winchester. "Jared's just so likeable," Kripke explains. As soon as they got the two Texan actors together, the camaraderie and chemistry was unmistakable. Ackles and Padalecki were everyone's first choice. "They're truly good, smart, down-to-earth guys," says Kripke, "and the bond that they have on camera is the bond they have off camera."

The pilot turned out great, and *Supernatural* got picked up for series. Since Kripke didn't have any show-running

experience, the studio partnered him with executive producer Bob Singer. "He's the great unsung hero of *Supernatural*," says Kripke of his producing partner. "He doesn't get a fraction of the credit he deserves. He's every bit a guiding creative force behind the show's direction as I am. He brings a depth of storytelling and a maturity that the show simply wouldn't have with just me. Left to my own devices I think I would have just made a really scary show and it would have had a lot of blood and gore. He's the one who's always saying, 'Whoa, whoa, slow down, what about the characters? What are they going through here?' A lot of that comes through in the brothers' relationship and that sort of mature yet sparse way they communicate with each other; they don't say much, but what they say means a lot. Most of that is Bob's influence."

The pilot was shot in Los Angeles, but for the second episode and beyond, the series moved to Vancouver, British Columbia, following in the footsteps of other atmospheric genre shows like *The X-Files* and *Dark Angel*. "The crew up there is amazing," Kripke says.

LEADING THE WAY: JARED PADALECKI

"Like Sam, I have an older brother," notes Jared Padalecki. "And Jensen has a brother, too, so we were both comfortable with that brotherly dynamic from the start. We're both Texans, as well. Jensen's laid back; he's a pretty relaxed guy. He and I just hit it off pretty quickly, really." It's a good thing, too, since as the only two leads on *Supernatural*, they were destined to work together pretty much all the time. Padalecki explains, "There were no other series regulars, which I've never heard of. Usually he and I—or if not both of us, then one of us—are working all day every day, which is really intense." That actually strengthened the actors' bond because, as Padalecki relates, "We knew we were both in this together."

Coming from the more straightforward *Gilmore Girls*, Padalecki didn't have much experience with visual effects, and he says, "A lot of times when there are visual effects and special effects, you don't have them there in front of you, so you're acting with nothing. I think it's a good thing to learn, and it's definitely an interesting skill to develop." One of his favorite visual effects, however, comes from scenes he wasn't in. "In the episode from season 3 called 'The Kids Are Alright,' when you see the little children who are actually changeling kids in a mirror and their faces are all gray and dead, that was scary to watch. I really enjoyed that episode, because it was really scary,

but also because I wasn't in that one much. Certain episodes are Sam heavy and others are Dean heavy, and since I wasn't in that one much I got to watch it as an audience member. I didn't know the story in great detail, so I was scared, I was laughing, and I was really happy with Jensen's performance."

There was one time, however, when Padalecki wasn't quite as happy with Ackles' performance. "It was during 'Mystery Spot' where we're talking at the same time," he says. "The line was, 'Sam Winchester wears makeup, Sam Winchester cries his way through sex, Sam Winchester keeps a ruler by the bed and every morning when he wakes up he—okay, enough!' But Jensen kept going from '. . . and every morning when he wakes up' to 'Okay, enough!' So he'd go to the 'okay' while I was still saying 'he.' We kept trying it and our crew was starting to laugh, but we couldn't break character, especially me, because once I start laughing, I'm done. So we'd keep making it through all the way to 'Sam Winchester keeps a ruler by the bed and every morning when he wakes up he . . .' and he'd just go straight to 'Okay, enough!' while I was going to 'he,' and we did that probably four or five times until finally I said, 'I'll change it, just tell me what you want.' Of course, inevitably I wouldn't say the 'he' because I was trying to do what he was doing, and on that take he would say it! We'd get so close. That was tough, but we got through it."

OPPOSITE AND ABOVE: Jared Padalecki's Sam Winchester has undergone quite a journey over the past seven seasons, and the younger Winchester now finds himself at a crucial crossroads in his career...

As tough as it was to mirror Ackles' words in that scene, Padalecki mentions another kind of mirror scene that was even tougher for him—the one where he had to play two characters talking to each other through one body. "It was very hard to do the mirror scenes when I was Sam and Lucifer. After having embodied this character for five years, it was tough to break into another character. I was happy I got to do it; any chance to explore a new character with new motivations is fun and exciting."

Even Soulless Sam? "Yes, definitely," he says. "It's really weird, though. Soulless Sam is the most different I've played from myself because as an actor you draw from your own experiences; and I hope I don't have anything to draw from that's sociopathic." Not that Padalecki actually made Soulless Sam a true sociopath. "I didn't want to be a socio-path," he continues, "because I didn't want to be inherently evil. The way I finally made it make sense in my mind is that someone who's soulless thinks purely rationally, so that if, say, these two people are going to kill those four people, is it better for four to die or better to kill two? It's almost like a mathematical question: 'What's better? Four to die or two to die?' Two to die! Even if they were innocent. It seems harsh, but I was soulless . . ."

Another character that required Padalecki to play someone very different from himself was when he had to depict a bad actor. "There's a scene in 'The French Mistake' where Sam and Dean were like, 'Uh, we better pretend we're actors.' We were doing such goofy things that Misha, Jensen, and I couldn't stop laughing. We were having so much fun!" Padalecki really enjoyed working on that episode. "I got to be married to my [real] wife, and we got to make fun of ourselves—when else are you going to get to do that? Unless it's a reality show about how you're messed up," he jokes. "I think the worst thing an actor can do is take himself too seriously, so I love the fact that we've been able to laugh at ourselves, not just with 'The French Mistake,' but with 'The Real Ghostbusters' and everything else."

The show's irreverent humor has helped ensure its continued success, and Padalecki is now going into his eighth season as Sam Winchester. "The show has changed so much," he reflects. "Jensen and I have grown up! It's been a growing process for everybody. The writers have paid attention to our portrayal of the characters over the years and have written to how we play them. Working with everyone on the show, all the writers, producers, and crew, has been a nice collaborative effort. It's like we all got on this winding road together and we just keep following it."

LEADING THE WAY: JENSEN ACKLES

You might think that playing a monster hunter on *Supernatural* would make you more attuned to detecting the real supernatural, but for Jensen Ackles, that isn't the case. "As far as ghosts and things that go bump in the night are concerned, I'm more of a logical, realist type," he says. "If something crashes in the living room in the middle of the night, I assume that the window was left open and the wind knocked the thing over as opposed to thinking some kind of ghostly spirit is wandering around the house." Fair enough, but what if there really *was* a monster in his house? "For that, *Supernatural* has probably given me a false sense of security," Ackles says with a chuckle. "I mean, I see a monster, I'm going to be like, 'Bring it on!'"

Maybe he did pick up some hunting instincts after all. Something else Ackles picked up while working on *Supernatural* was a knack for directing. "Being with the same crew for this long really allows you to explore a lot of different avenues," he says. In fact, he'd actually been thinking about directing right from season 1. "[Executive producer and director] Kim Manners was a very big motivating factor in pointing me in that direction," he says. "The level of respect I had for him, not only as a human but as a director, was very high, and I took a lot of mental notes when working with him. In season one, he said to me, 'You're going to direct one of these one day.' I remember when he said it

to me the first time, I was like, 'Yeah, *right*. Get outta here, I'm not going to direct, that's ridiculous.' Because I would see what he would do and say, 'I don't know how you do it.' But he believed in me. He said, 'When you direct—and you *will*—I've got three words for you: homework, homework, homework.' I took that into heavy consideration when I was prepping to direct 'Weekend at Bobby's.' There were some sleepless nights, and I basically had every shot thought out for the entire script before we even started day one of production. That's probably a little over-the-top as far as preparation goes, but I knew that if I had a plan, I could adjust it accordingly. Unless you're an amazing veteran of directing and you can shoot from the hip and hit the target every time, you've got to have a plan when you step on the set of a show. I had a plan, but I knew I could still shape it and evolve it, because obviously when you get to the set you want to lay out what you want to see, but you also want to leave the interpretation to the actors and let them bring their creativity as well."

Long before he directed his first episode in season 6, Ackles started reading the scripts with a director's eye. "I've found myself reading scripts and seeing it the way that I would want to see it on-screen, so in a sense I'm watching an edited film in my mind," he explains. "I probably started reading the

OPPOSITE AND ABOVE: Jensen Ackles has made the character of Dean Winchester his own over the course of seven seasons, including stepping behind the camera as director.

scripts like that around season 2 or so. Once I got a really good sense of the tone of the show and the tone of the characters, I was able to envision the way it was shot. It was really cool when I started reading scripts and seeing them play out in my mind, even seeing camera shots and stuff. That's when I realized, 'I'm actually directing the show in my mind right now.'" When he actually is directing, he utilizes the vision in his head from his script readings. "I just used the way I was reading it and the visions that were coming to me instinctually, and I would write those down and think, 'Okay, what do I need to accomplish that shot?' I'd think how to technically make that shot work, then I'd write it all down, and I'd draw little diagrams with stick figures. Directing is really fun, I enjoy it."

Even before "Weekend at Bobby's," Ackles got to direct his own scenes—sort of. In "Ghostfacers," due to the reality show conceit of the episode, he got to carry his own camera and choose his own marks. "I still had to be aware of the cameras, because obviously the other actors were holding cameras pointed at me, so I had to be aware, 'Okay, I have to say this line into this camera, then I gotta find this guy . . .' but there were no marks on the floor, there were no lights that we had to find, and it was a 360-degree set. I'm used to having a conversation with

fifteen crew guys standing within a ten-foot radius, but all those sets were closed. The technical aspect of acting is something that not a lot of people talk about, but I think it's crucial, especially for television, because of the pace that we film at. We had a lot of fun, and that episode turned out great."

It's too hard for Ackles to choose a favorite episode from all seven seasons, but he did narrow down his favorite season. "I really, really liked the first season, because for a lot of shows the first season involves finding out what they're doing and how they're doing it and which way they're going to go and maybe by the second season they have a better idea of it; but for this show, from the first season it was just *boom*! Right out of the gate we knew where we were headed, and we went there full force. I really liked how quickly the story developed in one season. And it was also just a lot of fun. I really liked season 4 as well. It was a tough season for Dean, which made it nice and challenging because even though it's more work, it's more rewarding. But as far as my favorite, I still love season 1 because of the monster-of-the-week formula—it was simple, it was tight. And I liked the fun nuances between the brothers. I understand that the show needs the mythology, and I applaud the writers for how they developed that, but I really like the monster-of-the-week episodes."

SEASON 1: THE STORY

On November 2, 1983, a baby named Sam Winchester is visited by a yellow-eyed demon that drips its blood into the infant's mouth. Sam's mother, Mary, tries to stop the demon, but is telekinetically pinned to the ceiling of the nursery. Hearing Mary scream, Sam's father, John, rushes in—but the demon is gone. Sam seems fine, but blood suddenly drips from the ceiling. John looks up and sees his bleeding wife erupt into flames! He orders his four-year-old son, Dean, to take Sam outside, and then attempts to save Mary. But it's too late, and John barely gets out of the house alive. John is devastated, and he becomes consumed by a smoldering rage, dedicating his life to finding the demon that killed his wife. He takes his sons on the road across America in his '67 Chevy Impala and sets his family on the path to becoming a clan of unstoppable monster hunters.

As they grow up, Sam and Dean come to share their father's goal of getting revenge on the Yellow-Eyed Demon, but they're also happy to kill any other evil creatures they encounter along the way. It's the perfect life for Dean: he's a good son and a good soldier. Sam, however, wants to be a lawyer and live a normal life. Having never known his mother, the younger Winchester brother's need for vengeance isn't as all-consuming as his father and brother's, so when he reaches the right age, Sam heads off to college. Unfortunately, his college days do not work out as planned. When John Winchester goes missing and Sam's girlfriend, Jessica Moore, is killed in the same horrific manner as his mother, Sam leaves the "normal" life behind to hunt alongside his brother.

But Sam and Dean's new life hunting together hits a few bumps in the road. Dean almost lets a demon kill a planeload of people because he's afraid to fly, while Sam's guilt over Jessica's death nearly gets them both killed by Bloody Mary. What's more, they barely escape with their skin intact when a murderous shapeshifter takes on Dean's likeness, and Sam nearly kills Dean while under the influence of the ghost of an insane asylum's doctor. Ultimately, though, they manage to work together successfully enough to gank all those monsters, banish some ghosts, and roast a wendigo, too.

OPPOSITE: Sam and Dean's journey as hunters started back in November of 1983, on a particularly harrowing night ... TOP LEFT: John Winchester says good night to his son Sam, never expecting that danger is just around the corner... ABOVE: Responding to his wife Mary's screams, John runs into the nursery to discover it—and his wife—on fire! TOP RIGHT: Mary's horrific fate at the hands of Azazel scars John Winchester forever. RIGHT: Years later, an adult Dean and Sam have become hunters in their own right, and now they must track down their missing father.

TOP: Dean lectures Sam on the rules of traveling in the Winchester car as he fills his beloved vehicle up with gas. ABOVE LEFT: When the brothers first reunite, there is still some lingering tension between them over the fact that Sam left the hunting life to go to college. ABOVE RIGHT: Dean's crippling fear of flying almost hinders the brothers' tracking down a demon onboard a deadly flight in "Phantom Traveler." OPPOSITE, TOP LEFT: Dean and Sam salt and burn a tracker's bones, but more danger awaits on "Route 666." OPPOSITE, TOP RIGHT: The skinwalker who took Dean's shape meets a grisly end. OPPOSITE, CENTER LEFT: Sam's encounter with Bloody Mary leaves him a little worse for the wear. OPPOSITE, CENTER RIGHT: Jensen and Jared take a break in between filming scenes for episode 103, "Dead in the Water." OPPOSITE, BOTTOM: Dean and Sam race to save another potential victim in "Dead in the Water."

Midway through their travels Sam starts to get psychic visions, and he fears he might be becoming some sort of freak himself. He admits to Dean that his visions started before Jessica died, that his dreams foretold what happened to her, and that he's burdened by the guilt he feels for not having warned her. His spirits are lifted when they discover that their father is alive, but Sam is confused when John warns him and Dean to stop looking for him. Ever the obedient soldier, Dean backs off, but Sam disagrees. Splitting with his brother to chase John down, he encounters a drifter named Meg. Dean, meanwhile, gets in a bind with a vanir (a nature and fertility god requiring human sacrifices), causing Sam to race back to the rescue, leaving Meg behind. This turns out to be a good thing, since she's a demon spying on the Winchesters for her father Azazel—the Yellow-Eyed Demon.

The brothers decide to stick together, realizing they truly need each other. Especially when Dean's heart gets damaged battling a rawhead (an Irish boogeyman feared by children) and Sam doesn't rest until he finds a preacher "miraculously"

saving people's lives with the help of a leashed reaper. Or when Dean rescues Sam from a family of cannibals. Or when they work together to fight off Meg's daevas (destructive, invisible beings who rip humans apart) and exorcise her back to Hell.

The brothers eventually track down their father, and it's all (awkward) hugs and vampire slaying at first, but then the Yellow-Eyed Demon possesses John and things spiral out of control. Dean is tortured by Azazel, who, ironically, is furious because Dean killed his son, the demon known as Tom. While the Yellow-Eyed Demon is distracted by Dean, Sam gets hold of the Colt—a magical weapon capable of killing supernatural creatures—but he can't bring himself to kill the demon since it would mean killing his father as well. Instead, he shoots John in the leg, expelling Azazel. The Yellow-Eyed Demon is not done with them yet, however. As Sam drives his father and brother to the hospital, a semitruck driven by a demon-possessed driver smashes into the car, injuring John and Sam and leaving Dean on the verge of death . . .

OPPOSITE: Dean and Sam learn that their father is indeed alive, but that he does not wish to see them ... TOP LEFT: Dean and Sam encounter a reaper in "Faith." TOP RIGHT: When Sam and Dean finally catch up with their father, John seems to be acting strangely ... CENTER LEFT: Turns out John is being possessed by the Yellow-Eyed Demon and wants to destroy the Winchesters before they can kill him. ABOVE LEFT: An injured Sam must decide whether to use the Colt to kill Azazel— and probably John Winchester in the process. ABOVE RIGHT: Dean is unsure of what the future holds once he and Sam are reunited with their father ...

ABOVE LEFT AND RIGHT: John Winchester and Mary Campbell: Lovers and future hunters.

JOHN AND MARY WINCHESTER: SPOUSES, PARENTS, HUNTERS

Once upon a time there was a dashing knight named John Winchester and a fair maiden named Mary Campbell. They met, fell in love, had children, defended their family from an evil monster, and lived happily ever after. Well, not exactly—here's the *real* story:

John Winchester married the love of his life, Mary Campbell, and they had two sons, Dean and Sam—but that's where the fairy tale ends and the nightmare begins. Enter Azazel, the Yellow-Eyed Demon, who murders Mary in Sam's nursery. Seeking vengeance, John devotes his life to hunting the demon. What he doesn't realize is that he's encountered the supernatural twice before. On the night he proposed to Mary Campbell, the Yellow-Eyed Demon killed him and then brought him back to life without any memory of the incident. Plus, when Mary was pregnant with Dean, John was nearly killed by the angel Anna, before being possessed by the Archangel Michael, after which his memories of the events were erased.

John hunts the Yellow-Eyed Demon relentlessly and obsessively, raising his sons in the monster-hunting life in the process. When he finally catches up with his nemesis, the demon possesses him. Sam shoots his father with the mystical Colt pistol, driving the demon out. John is angry Sam didn't aim to kill. To John's way of thinking, killing this demon comes first—before him, before everything.

Later, one of Azazel's minions possesses a truck driver and smashes into the Winchesters' beloved car, injuring all three of them. Dean's injuries are life-threatening, so John trades his soul and the Colt to Azazel in exchange for the demon agreeing to save Dean's life. But later, after the Devil's Gate in Wyoming is opened, Dean gets the Colt back and John escapes Hell, helping his sons kill the Yellow-Eyed Demon before he disappears, never to be seen again.

Mary Winchester, née Campbell, lived a life of adventure before she met John. Her parents, Samuel and Deanna Campbell, were hunters, as were most of her family before her, stretching back generations. Mary keeps her past secret from John for fear of losing him, or worse. Her fears are well warranted; the night John proposes to her is also the night the Yellow-Eyed Demon kills John *and* her parents. As a result, Mary gives the Yellow-Eyed Demon permission to enter her home ten years in the future in exchange for saving John's life in the present. This deal inadvertently provides the demon access to baby Sam, to whom he feeds his blood in preparation for Sam to eventually become Lucifer's vessel on Earth.

TOP AND ABOVE: John Winchester's single-minded pursuit of the Yellow-Eyed Demon that killed his wife, Mary, turned him into a formidable hunter, but it also led him to have a strained and difficult relationship with his sons. ABOVE RIGHT: Mary Winchester gave up the hunting life when she married John, but ten years after their wedding, the Yellow-Eyed Demon arrived to collect on his past deal with her ...

Years later, when Sam and Dean are adults, the angel Anna wants to stop Lucifer from walking the Earth in his chosen vessel and starting the Apocalypse, so she goes back to the past and tries to kill John Winchester so that Sam will never be born. Mary comes to her husband's rescue, however, then shocks John by revealing that monsters are real and that she has been hunting them ever since she was a little girl. But she's in for a shock of her own when her grown sons also time travel to save Mary from Anna. In the end, it's the Archangel Michael that saves them all, but he also erases Mary's memory of everything that happened, including Dean's warning not to go into Sam's nursery on the night the Yellow-Eyed Demon visits.

Which, of course, she does, and the Yellow-Eyed Demon, not liking to be interrupted, telekinetically pins her to the ceiling and sets her on fire! Guilt-ridden over what happened to Sam, Mary's spirit clings to the house, but John takes Sam and Dean on the road, never to return. That is, until twenty-two years later, when Sam has nightmares about his old home, leading him and Dean to investigate. But a poltergeist has moved in, and it tries to kill Mary's boys. She saves them by dragging the malevolent spirit away to another realm, and like her husband, she is never seen again.

Adam, the Unknown Winchester

Adam Milligan is the son of Kate Milligan and John Winchester, but Adam didn't meet his father until he was twelve. Even then, John kept his "day job" a secret from his youngest son. Adam discovered the existence of supernatural monsters the hard way: a ghoul ate him and took on his identity. Adam was a student at Wisconsin University when he died, and his upbringing was far removed from the hunting life his half-brothers Sam and Dean lived. Nevertheless, they still wound up having a lot in common, such as a penchant for sarcasm and being hounded by angels keen to turn him into an archangel's vessel. At first Adam thought it would be cool to team up with an archangel to stop the Apocalypse, but by the time Zachariah showed Adam how merciless most angels are, it was too late. Adam became Michael's vessel, and he remains trapped with Lucifer and Michael in Lucifer's cage in Hell.

THE WINCHESTERS' WHEELS

The Winchesters' Impala is an automatic, four-door hardtop with a black exterior that does double duty as both stylish transportation and sleeping quarters for Sam and Dean Winchester. There is no doubt that it is now Dean's "baby," but it was originally owned by Sal Moriarty (who loaded it up with Bibles instead of weapons). Paradoxically, John Winchester purchased the Winchester car from a used car lot at the insistence of his time-traveling future son, Dean. When Sam and Dean were kids, one of them crammed a toy soldier into the ashtray, and they slipped some Lego bricks into the vents, which still rattle around to this day.

The car is perfect for hunting because the trunk can hold a massive weapons arsenal, two duffel bags of clothes, *and* a body (human or monster). More importantly, it has a cassette player radio—iPod jacks are *not* welcome. Regarding the latter, Dean has one golden rule: the driver always, always, always picks the music, and shotgun shuts his cakehole.

This poor car has been possessed by the ghosts of Rose Brown and Constance Welch (the latter also known as the Woman in White), and taken beatings from a demon-driven semitruck and a hurricane-force cloud of unleashed demons. But it's the relentless tracking of the Leviathan that truly decommissioned it for the better part of a year. Because the Leviathan disguised themselves as Sam and Dean, and the Winchesters were known to drive the distinctive car, the brothers were forced to put the beloved car in storage until the threat was over. During that time, Dean and Sam were forced to drive many impostors: an AMC Pacer, a Buick Riviera, a Buick Special Deluxe, a Dodge Challenger, a Dodge Charger, a Mercury Cougar, a Pontiac Acadian, and a Pontiac Firebird. Now the car is in Sam's hands again, until Dean claws his way out of Purgatory, if for no other reason than to get back in the driver's seat where he belongs.

The Car's Weapons Cache

"The weapons cache in the Winchesters' car is all over the place," comments property master Christopher Cooper. "It's chaos, Dean Winchester-style."

"For the record, the car's trunk is Felix's bag of tricks," states creator Eric Kripke, referencing the magic bag that took on any form desired by the titular character in the 1950s cartoon *Felix the Cat*. "There isn't anything that Sam and Dean can't magically reach into that trunk and pull out," he says. "You may not have seen it before, but you totally believe it's in there. It's a cheat for us, but it's a really useful cheat. We can pull anything we want out of that trunk and it's credible."

There are countless things hidden in the weapon cache, and many more things that will magically appear when the story calls for them, but take a close look at what's in there pretty much all the time. You'll spot Sam and Dean's favorite handguns, the flare gun used in "Wendigo," the stake used to "kill" the Trickster in "Tall Tales," and a knife passed down to Dean from John Winchester.

AFTERMARKET
ACCESSORIES

- shotguns
- rifles
- pistols
- axe
- holy water
- dream catcher
- rosary
- knives
- assorted blades
- wooden stakes
- hex bags

UNDER THE HOOD

- The show uses four cars, plus junkers for spare parts.
- Enhancements: All the brakes have been converted from old drum brakes to four-wheel disc brakes. They use two high-performance cars that have Chevy 250 engines with cams and four-barrel carburetors.
- The stunt cars have a stomp break—which locks the rear wheels to swing them into skids—and a control to lock the front brakes so they can burn rubber with the back wheels.
- According to transport coordinator Mark Gould, "That car's never seen on-camera dirty, ever, unless that's how [the writers and directors] want it."

OPPOSITE, TOP: The sleek black car Dean inherited from his father John, which has been lovingly customized by both Winchesters over the years. OPPOSITE, BOTTOM: One of the unique customizations of the car Dean drives is the weapons cache hidden in the trunk. It is a one-stop shop of hunter's tools that have aided the Winchesters for over seven years now. TOP AND ABOVE: Two views of the car and its famous occupants being filmed, the top from season 3 and the bottom from the pilot. The car has become such an iconic part of Supernatural *that it is in essence the third Winchester.*

THINGS THAT GO BUMP IN THE NIGHT

 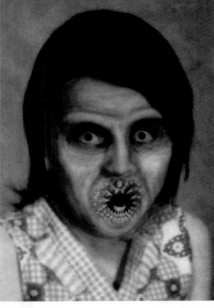 

ABOVE LEFT: The Antichrist looks innocent but is deadly powerful. ABOVE CENTER: A changeling child is anything but cute and cuddly. ABOVE RIGHT: Not all ghosts are evil, and are often the restless spirits of loved ones recently departed.

SUPERNATURAL'S MONSTERS

The horrifying truth is that there are too many monsters lurking around every corner to count, much less describe in detail, but what follows is an A-to-Z primer on the most supernatural beings Dean and Sam have encountered in the past seven years . . .

ANTICHRIST

Description: Born of a demon-possessed virgin human, the Antichrist is possessed of almost limitless supernatural abilities, and can destroy the "Host of Heaven" with a single word. After Lucifer is raised, the Antichrist's abilities grow even more powerful.

Behavior: The Antichrist's powers include telekinesis, teleportation, exorcising demons with his mind, and making even the simplest of thoughts a reality.

Hunting Tip: The Antichrist is impossible to kill, but can be persuaded to never use his powers again if reasoned with compassionately.

CHANGELINGS

Description: A supernatural creature that mimics the appearance and behavior of human children in order to feed off of their mothers.

Behavior: Changeling children will kill anyone who tries to keep them away from feeding on their human mothers, while the changeling mother takes care of feeding the human children who have been abducted and replaced.

Hunting Tip: Changelings can be destroyed by fire, and when the changeling mother is killed, her brood dies with her.

DJINN (GENIES)

Description: Essentially evil genies, djinn are creatures of smokeless fire, but their solid human form is indistinguishable from regular humans.

Behavior: With just a touch, they make their victim's greatest wish come true, but only inside their victims' minds. These supernatural hallucinations feel so real the victims rarely try to wake up, which is the point, since while they're in dreamland the djinn feeds off their bodily fluids.

Hunting Tip: Djinn can be killed with a silver knife dipped in lamb's blood.

GHOSTS

Description: Spirits of the deceased that are trapped on Earth.

Behavior: They can walk through walls, the stronger ones can move objects and kill people, and they'll haunt just about anything—loved ones, houses, hotels, mental asylums, cars, boats, roads, flasks—and some ghosts can even infect people like a disease, making them so afraid of everything that their hearts burst.

Hunting Tip: They're usually tethered to their bones, so if they've been cremated, look for other remains of theirs that would have some DNA attached, like a friendship bracelet with blood on it or a wig made out of their hair, or even a donated kidney.

GHOULS

Description: Monster scavengers that eat the dead and take on the likeness, thoughts, and memories of their last meal.

Behavior: Most of the time they dig up graves and eat the corpses, but if they are disturbed or angry enough they'll come after the living, too. Once they've tasted fresh meat, however, they're not likely to go back to a cemetery anytime soon.

Hunting Tip: They can only be killed by decapitation or the destruction of their heads.

"KHAN WORM"

Description: One of Eve, the Mother of All Monsters' creations, a parasitic worm that crawls into humans' ears and takes control of their bodies. It was dubbed "Khan worm" by Dean Winchester.

Behavior: Takes evil pleasure in turning friends and family against each other with deadly consequences, and was a tool developed and tested by Eve as a means of exterminating humankind.

Hunting Tip: If you suspect a Khan worm's in the room, don't let anyone out of your sight. It can be killed with electrical current.

PAGAN GODS

Description: Supernatural entities that gain their power from humans worshipping them as gods.

Behavior: They like to eat humans, but they're not greedy; they provide their worshippers with bountiful harvests, good health, and protection from other hungry pagan gods in return for a relatively small number of human sacrifices.

Hunting Tip: If you feel compelled to tell the truth, the whole truth, and nothing but the truth, chances are Veritas is working her magic. If you're feeling guilty about something you did, you had better watch out for Osiris or he'll pass a death sentence on you. And watch out for creepy scarecrows—they could be vanir in disguise.

REAPERS

Description: A spirit-like creature that nowadays usually appears in human form (ranging from a pretty young woman to a shriveled old man), but historically was known as a skeletal figure carrying a large scythe and wearing a long, hooded black robe.

Behavior: They reap souls for Death. They can stop time and alter human perception, and will use sweet talk, scare tactics, or any other methods they can think of to get the newly dead to cross over to the afterlife.

Hunting Tip: The living can't see them, so you have to use astral projection or kill yourself in order to find them. Better yet, use an angel—or if you're desperate, a demon—as your go-between, as they can see reapers easily.

ABOVE LEFT: The scarecrow is a minor pagan god. ABOVE CENTER: The reaper Tessa is unswerving in her unenviable job of shepherding the newly dead to the afterlife. ABOVE RIGHT: Shapeshifters can often take the shape of anything they see or notice, including classic movie characters!

ABOVE LEFT: Shtriga are as dangerous as they are scary looking. ABOVE CENTER: Werewolves are real, and this one is almost ready for his close-up, thanks to the prosthetics department. ABOVE RIGHT: Wendigo crave human flesh and live in the dark to avoid being spotted in the daylight.

SHAPESHIFTERS/SKINWALKERS

Description: A monster with the ability to transform into an exact replica of a human or an animal.

Behavior: They study your routines and mannerisms, then take on your appearance and psychically steal your memories to mimic you perfectly. Depending on what they want, they'll often take over your life while you're away from home, then when they're ready to move on, or if you discover them, they'll kill you and make it look like a suicide. Some can simply change their appearance, while others must actually shed their old skins when their new form emerges.

Hunting Tip: All shapeshifters/skinwalkers can be killed with a silver bullet (or other sharp silver object) to the heart.

SHTRIGA

Description: A ghastly-looking soul-sucker; some lore says they start off as witches.

Behavior: Shtriga are a type of witch that feed by sucking the "breath of life," or *spiritus vitae*, out of people. They prefer children because their life forces are strongest, but any human will do. They target sick, suicidal, or otherwise weak people because their life forces are not attached as strongly to their bodies.

Hunting Tip: They take on the guise of humans, often working in hospitals and old-age homes. They're creatures of habit, so check old photos to see if any health care workers haven't aged in decades. Shtriga don't like to be disturbed when they're feeding, preferring to sneak about quietly, meaning they target unlocked doors and windows. They can only be killed by consecrated wrought iron.

SIRENS

Description: Mythology-rooted creatures that have pale skin, hollow eyes, and a scary mouth, but they usually take on human form.

Behavior: They can read minds and use what they learn to take on the guise of someone their intended victims will desire being with, then they use their supernaturally toxic saliva to turn their victims into adoring slaves.

Hunting Tip: The only way to kill a siren is with a bronze dagger dipped in the blood of someone it has infected.

VAMPIRES

Description: "Turned" humans with extra-sharp, retractable teeth that crave human blood.

Behavior: They nest in packs and sleep in cocoon-style hammocks, not coffins. They need to feed on mammalian blood to survive, and human blood tastes the best. However, animal blood—from rats, cows, pigs, cats, dogs—will suffice. They sire new vampires by force-feeding people their infected blood.

Hunting Tip: The smell of your blood will warn vampires that you're coming, so if you're trying to sneak up on them, make a broth with skunk cabbage, saffron, and trillium, and after it cools, splash it all over yourself. Crosses do not repel them, and direct sunlight burns them but does not kill them, nor will a stake through the heart. Vampires can only be killed through beheading.

WENDIGO

Description: An individual who has eaten human flesh in conjunction with black magic and gained inhuman speed and strength, as well as immortality. They're bigger than humans, and their teeth and nails have grown monstrously long.

Behavior: Lures hikers deep into the forest, sometimes using their own stolen equipment as bait, then holds them prisoner in its underground lair until feeding time.

Hunting Tip: If you're looking for a wendigo in a dark place, you can spot them by their glowing eyes. They can only be killed with fire.

WEREWOLVES

Description: A person infected by lycanthropy who turns into a ravenous, supernaturally strong human-wolf hybrid during the full moon.

Behavior: Although they act like feral animals, werewolves tend to hunt and kill people who have angered them in their human lives. If it wasn't for this connection, they might never find out they're werewolves, as they don't seem to retain any memories of their monstrous behavior.

Hunting Tip: Whatever you do, don't get bitten. Don't listen to hunters who tell you that killing the werewolf that bit you will lift the curse, as there is no cure. Werewolves can only be killed by a silver bullet.

WITCHES

Description: Humans who use dark magic to perform curses, summon demons, and even swap bodies.

Behavior: Witches need to use various combinations of spells, sigils, effigies, hex bags, and animal sacrifices to affect others magically. They usually use their magic to enrich their own lives and torture their enemies.

Hunting Tip: A dead rabbit strung up in an otherwise luxurious home is a clue a witch lives there. Witches can be killed using conventional weapons.

WRAITHS

Description: A humanoid creature that gets close to other humans in order to eat their brains. A wraith has a spike that pops out of its wrist when it's feeding.

Behavior: They enjoy the taste of "insane" brains and are usually found near mental institutions. They are capable of causing hallucinations and other emotional changes through physical touch.

Hunting Tip: If you're having trouble killing a wraith, lock it up; they'll die if they go too long without feeding on human flesh. They can also be killed with a weapon made of pure silver.

ZOMBIES

Description: A dead person reanimated by Death or through necromancy.

Behavior: They will often try to go back to their old lives, but are driven by a hunger for revenge and will happily kill anyone who wronged them in life. They seem normal at first—happy, even—but eventually they will crave human flesh and the hunger will escalate, turning them into a stereotypical zombie.

Hunting Tips: The residual magic from zombie risings causes plants in their immediate vicinity to die. They can be killed by staking, beheading, or otherwise destroying their heads.

ABOVE LEFT: Witches often look like they do in old fairy tales and movies, and nine times out of ten they are indeed very, very wicked … ABOVE CENTER: Wraiths' teeth are just as sharp as the spikes that protrude from their wrists when it's time to feed. ABOVE RIGHT: Zombies are simply the dead reanimated for various reasons and purposes, and often can be loved ones you never thought you'd see again …

A HUNTER'S TOOLS

WHAT YOU NEED TO GANK A MONSTER EFFECTIVELY

AXE—An essential weapon for a hunter, as it can be used to decapitate monsters (such as vampires and Leviathan—creatures created by God and imprisoned due to their unstable nature).

BAMBOO DAGGER—Kills okami (fanged Japanese monsters who feed on humans) if it's properly blessed by a Shinto priest, but the monster must be stabbed exactly seven times, or it is not truly dead.

BLOOD—Dead man's blood poisons vampires; dog's blood poisons some pagan gods (like Veritas, the Goddess of Truth); dragon's blood is needed to kill dragons; lamb's blood is needed to kill djinn. Blood is also an essential ingredient in most summoning and/or banishment spells.

BRASS (blades, steam organ pipes, etc.)—Kills rakshasa (shapeshifting demons who feed on human flesh) and also has repelling properties.

BRONZE BLADE—Kills sirens, primarily, but it is also a convenient weapon when dealing with "regular" monsters.

CAMERA—Flash will briefly immobilize creatures that are used to the dark; the viewfinder reveals ghosts and the flare in shapeshifters' or other types of monsters' eyes.

CHAIN SAW—Decapitates most monsters, and will momentarily incapacitate just about any creature until it can be killed.

CREAM—Inebriates faeries, according to ancient lore and to firsthand experience by Dean and Sam Winchester.

CROSSBOW—Depends on the supernatural strength of the monsters, but regular projectile usage applies.

CURSE BOXES—Keeps cursed objects from affecting those who handle the boxes. Essential when dealing with magical items, but must be locked properly.

ELECTROMAGNETIC FIELD (EMF) METER—Locates ghosts and is perhaps one of the most essential tools a hunter can have in his or her arsenal. Most are homemade.

FIRE (blowtorches, disposable lighters, flare guns, matches, etc.)—Kills changelings, crocotta (creatures that take human form to feed on humans' souls), ghouls, rougarous (flesh-eating monsters), and wendigos. Fire is a natural tool for hunters, given that most creatures are susceptible to it.

GUN (handguns, shotguns, sniper rifles, etc.)—Slows down just about any monster and, with the proper ammo, can also kill them. Regular bullets can kill Amazons, witches, ghouls, and zombies.

HEX BAG—Hides the bearer from demons. Can also be used to wreak havoc if hidden in a person's home, vehicle, or clothing.

HOLY WATER—Harms and repels demons. Can be used by direct application, or if weapons are wet with the blessed liquid.

IRIDIUM (axes, bullets, knives, swords, etc.)—Kills alpha monsters. As alpha monsters are rare and hard to kill, it is essential that your iridium-forged weapon is clean and sharp.

IRON (axes, buckshot, bullets, chains, knives, nails, etc.)—Dispels ghosts; keeps demons, faeries, and phoenixes (creatures who turn their victims to ash) at bay or traps them; and kills shtriga and some pagan gods (like leshii).

KNIFE—Depends on the supernatural strength of the monster, but regular blade usage applies. A standard weapon for every hunter's arsenal.

LOCK PICKS—Their use is self-explanatory, but they are essential tools of the trade for hunters, so it is important to keep quite a few in various shapes and sizes handy.

MACHETE—Ideal for decapitating monsters (such as arachne), as well as vampires and Leviathan.

MIRROR—Shows the true faces of changelings, sirens, and wraiths, and is a good tool to quickly discover the real nature of anybody you suspect to be a monster in disguise.

PALO SANTO (Holy Wood)—Toxic to demons and serves the same purpose as holy water in repelling or harming—but not killing—these creatures of Satan.

RAM'S HORN—Kills some pagan gods (like Osiris) and can often be found in synagogues.

SALT—Circles of salt and salt lines across entryways keep out ghosts and demons. Shotgun blasts of rock salt dispel ghosts.

SILVER (axes, bullets, knives, stakes, swords, etc.)—Kills djinn, shapeshifters, skinwalkers, vetala (creatures that sedate their victims with a toxin and feed on them for days), wendigos, werewolves, wraiths, and zombies. Having silver on hand when facing most monsters and creatures is essential.

SUGAR—When sugar is spilled in front of them, faeries have to stop what they're doing and count every grain.

SWORD—Perfect for decapitating monsters (such as Leviathan); kills dragons (when coated in dragon's blood); and kills shojo sea spirits (when consecrated by a Shinto blessing).

TASER—Electrocutes rawheads, but is also handy for incapacitating a variety of monsters or even belligerent humans.

WOODEN STAKE (Babylonian cypress, evergreen, etc.)—Kills pagan gods, the Whore of Bablylon, and tricksters.

OPPOSITE, TOP LEFT: Blood is an essential ingredient in most spells and rituals. OPPOSITE, BOTTOM LEFT: Dean's distinctive EMF reader remains the Winchesters' most essential hunting tool. OPPOSITE, RIGHT: A phone camera allows Sam to spot all of Eve's monsters in the diner where the Winchesters confront her. TOP LEFT: Salting and burning the physical remains of a person or their effects is the only way to banish a ghost for good. TOP RIGHT: Rifles, handguns, pistols, and shotguns are all essential weapons for a professional hunter. ABOVE LEFT: While harder to find than more ordinary weapons, real swords (not fake replicas) are also effective when hunting certain monsters and creatures. ABOVE RIGHT: Wooden stakes are easy to make and invaluable for slaying all those creatures that need their hearts, or other major organs, pierced.

BEHIND THE SCENES

WRITERS AND PRODUCERS

Executive producer Sera Gamble has lived the dream of many Hollywood writers: she started as a staff writer and steadily worked her way up to showrunner. As a talented writer she had more than one job opportunity during 2005's pilot season, and she shares why she chose *Supernatural*. "I watched the pilot and thought it was really, *really* cool," she says. "There were a lot of supernatural-themed shows and science fiction shows that season, but I had the very strong sense that *Supernatural* was the one that was going to last. It had the clearest franchise, and it really knew exactly what it wanted to be tonally. It was very attractive to me to be a part of a show that really knew what it was."

It was, of course, a show about two brothers fighting creatures of legend. Initially, the stories were created with the urban legends and supernatural creatures dominating the show, and the brothers' story was secondary. The focus shifted in the second season, as executive producer John Shiban explains. "First season, nine times out of ten we started with

the monster," he says. "At the start of the second season, Eric Kripke said, 'I want to hear monsters, but I also want to hear situations and dramatic problems for the characters. Bring those in first. If you have a good situation, we'll find a monster for it.'"

"That sprung out of just wanting to spend more time with Sam and Dean, with their problems," notes creator Eric Kripke. "The more we did that, the more the mythology started taking on a mind of its own. To use an example, in the universe of the original *Star Wars* trilogy you have this massive Rebellion, you have this massive Empire, but the story is through the eyes of this farmboy, this pirate, and this princess."

The character-first focus has remained, but the monsters and legends are equally important, and often episodes still come from myth-first pitches. "'I Believe the Children Are Our Future' was one of those episodes where we started with the kills and then came up with a reason," Kripke reveals. "We started with how we wanted all the lies that parents tell children to come true. That was the notion that [Daniel Loflin and Andrew Dabb] pitched, that Pop Rocks and Coke would cause your stomach to explode, that joy buzzers could kill you, that the Tooth Fairy was real—all of those things. And we wanted to really tell a story about how the way that people lie to children isn't necessarily a bad thing, and that the motivation behind it is to keep them safe and protected. That was where we started, and then we said, 'What would allow us to have that story within the apocalyptic pantheon [of season 5]?' We started looking at the Antichrist. We thought it would be a really intriguing notion for us to have an Antichrist who is generally a likeable kid that's making all of these childish things come to life simply because he doesn't know any better."

Similarly, in season 6, co–executive producer Adam Glass enjoyed exploring the notion of "finding the things that are woven into the fabric of our society, like having a baby ["Two and a Half Men"] or having a family dog ["All Dogs Go to Heaven"]. What struck truest were simple, relatable ideas," he explains. "And then expanding on those ideas an saying, 'Okay, well, what if the family dog was the monster in your house but it loves you? Yet, what if there's another plan for it, where it's supposed to turn the family it fell in love with into monsters, too? Let's start thinking about thi sympathetic monster's motivation.' Basically it was a choic between two families. Which family do you choose: the family that made you or the family that loves and takes car of you? For us, that's really rich and interesting stuff to explore. I love the idea of taking this thing that you think one thing, but showing that it has a heart and soul, showin that it has compassion, showing that things are not so black-and-white, and just swimming in that gray area, whi to me is always where the most interesting characters are."

Which brings up the question: what qualifies as a monster? Regular humans can do monstrous things; just look at the Benders or any serial killer. But those people a defined by their behavior. What about humans with psych powers? Do the powers make the person a monster? Pame

OPPOSITE, LEFT: Series creator, writer, and director Eric Kripke. OPPOSITE, RIGHT: The much-loved late director, Kim Manners. ABOVE LEFT: Former showrunner and executive producer Sera Gamble. ABOVE RIGHT: Executive producer and director Bob Singer with actor Jensen Ackles.

WRITE WHAT YOU KNOW?

Does creator Eric Kripke believe in the stuff he writes about, the real supernatura He says, "I have to admit that I'm skeptical. I've become more skeptical of the supernatural since doing this show. When you work on this show day in and day and your daily job is monsters and spirits, they lose a little bit of their mystery, they lose a little bit of their luster. When you watch dailies of a creature acting and then someone calls cut and you take a sip of your Diet Coke and want to k where Craft Services is, it kind of detracts from the illusion of it. But I hope it' there; I want to have an experience. I want to believe in this stuff …"

nes would certainly say no. And even though Max ler used his psychic powers irresponsibly in ghtmare," his father and uncle were themselves human nsters, so some viewers might have balked at Sam and an killing psychic Max. "We don't ever want Sam and an to kill a human 'just because,'" confirms Gamble. tead, Max killed himself, which former writer Raelle ker calls "Hardcore. We had to fight really hard to keep t moment in."

nother hardcore scene, at least for its effect on the otions of the fans, was when Sam failed to save Dean n being torn apart by Hellhounds and the elder nchester actually went to Hell. That wasn't supposed to pen. But twelve episodes into the production of season here was a writers' strike in Hollywood. Fortunately, e was enough time to continue the season after the ke ended, but not a lot. Instead of having ten more odes to tell the rest of the season's overarching storyline, were reduced to just four episodes.

all got back into the writers' room to decide how we going to wrap the season, and we quickly realized that

a storyline about Sam's abilities, which we had been planning on, was going to have to wait for season 4," says Kripke, "and that the story to expand and accelerate was Dean's deal. The original version was going to be Dean *about to* go to Hell, and then in the eleventh hour Sam was going to use his dark demonic powers to stop Lilith and *save* Dean."

"People are jaded toward the expected scares," points out executive producer Ben Edlund, "so it's a good challenge to try to scare people, to catch them off-guard, somehow— whether it's with a bit of quirky irreverence or by shaking up their expectations." As shocking as the decision to actually send Dean to Hell was, it set a precedent of fearlessness in the writers' room that has taken the show to many wild and wonderful places ever since. "The emphasis since the start of season 4 has been to take the *Supernatural* formula—two guys come to town, there's a monster, they fight the monster, they defeat the monster—and twist it up," points out co–executive producer Andrew Dabb. "For the writers, creatively, it's really awesome," Glass says. "You can sit down and think of anything; there is no ceiling on it. There are no boundaries!"

A Tribute to Kim Manners

"I knew when I read the pilot script that it was good," Jensen Ackles reflects. "And I knew when we started working on the pilot that this show had a really good shot at being successful. I was confident in it and I was also excited about it, but I think the moment that I knew it was going to have legs was probably after Kim Manners directed his first episode. He had done nine seasons of *The X-Files*, and I'd never worked with a force like him. He had so much talent and so much respect from the crew that I instantly thought, 'If this guy can man the helm, we're going to go places.' I remember I called Eric Kripke and said, 'I know you guys were trying to get an in-house director to run the show in Vancouver, and I think Kim Manners is your guy.' And Eric responded, 'We already got him.' Right then I knew, 'this show has got legs.' "

During the fourth season, the beloved executive producer and gifted director was diagnosed with lung cancer. "Metamorphosis" was the last episode he directed, and he passed away on January 25, 2009. "In the middle of shooting through amazingly difficult hours and hard production days, people were trying to deal with and internalize that loss, and it was just remarkably difficult," creator Eric Kripke recalls sadly.

On behalf of the crew, lead makeup artist Shannon Coppin eulogized, "Kim Manners was the glue that held us all together. We miss you, Kim!"

CHAPTER 2

OPENING THE DEVIL'S GATE

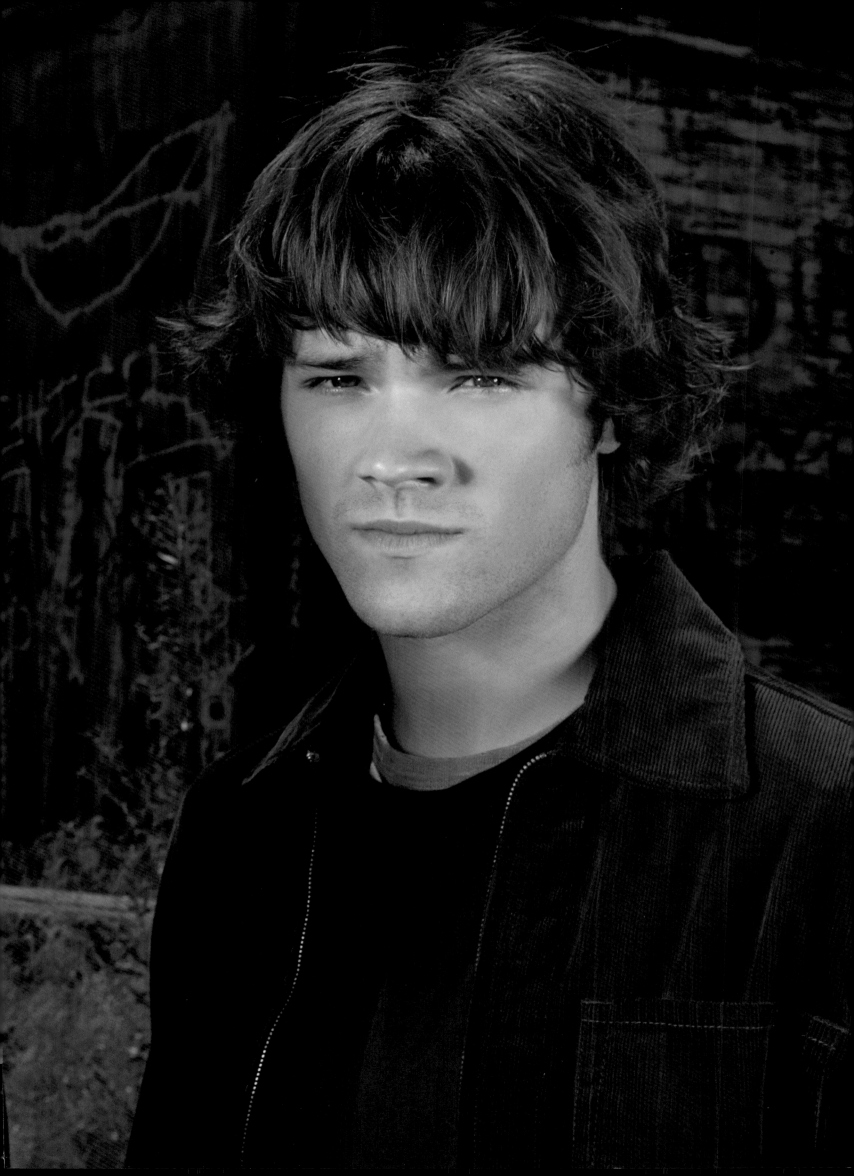

SEASON 2: THE STORY

Following the crash, Dean Winchester barely makes it out of the wreckage alive, and, once he's in the hospital, things look bleak for him. On the verge of death, his spirit leaves his body, and he encounters a reaper named Tessa who tries to convince him to let go of the mortal world and die. Believing Dean's death is imminent, John Winchester makes a deal with the Yellow-Eyed Demon, trading his life—and the Colt—for Dean's. Before the demon takes him to Hell, John tells a now-healed Dean that he has to save Sam from turning evil, or else he'll be forced to kill his younger brother.

John's death leads Sam to let go of his lingering doubts about being a hunter, and he tells Dean he is now committed to their mission. Their primary goal: find and kill the Yellow-Eyed Demon. Along the way, they spend time with their surrogate uncle, Bobby Singer, and get to know more of John's friends, namely Ellen Harvelle, her daughter Jo, and computer genius Ash. The usual ghosts and demons don't faze the brothers, nor does an encounter with a zombie, but it's hard for Sam to

concentrate on tracking the Yellow-Eyed Demon when clowns scare him, "good" vampires confuse him, a hot werewolf entices him, and unstable hunter Gordon Walker hunts him. It is revealed that Sam possesses demonic psychic powers, which explains John's cryptic warning to Dean. It also explains why Gordon has jumped to the conclusion that Sam is now irredeemably evil. Fortunately, Sam's sinister abilities make him immune to the other psychic children's powers, and also render him immune to the Croatoan virus, a plague developed by demons to turn humans into mindless, flesh-eating savages.

His new powers, however, fail to make Sam feel any better about the fact that his own father believed he was capable of crossing over to the dark side. What's more, John's fears seem to be coming true when Sam temporarily becomes an evil monster when he's possessed by the demon Meg. He kills another hunter—and nearly kills Jo and Dean, too.

Dean finds it hard to cope with both his brother's unstable condition and the guilt over his father's sacrifice as he attempts

OPPOSITE: Sam and his father John argue about Dean's dire medical prognosis while Dean's spirit tries to communicate with his family. TOP LEFT: Hunter and computer genius Ash is an invaluable—and quirky—ally to Sam and Dean as they investigate a series of cases. ABOVE LEFT: Disposing of ghosts, zombies, monsters, and other creatures is hard physical labor, no matter how simple the hunt may be. LEFT: A tense standoff between hunter Gordon and Sam over a benevolent vampire leads to more problems for the Winchesters down the road. TOP RIGHT: Dean's first meeting with Jo Harvelle is less than friendly ... CENTER RIGHT: The Winchesters encounter their first case of zombies in episode 204, "Children Shouldn't Play with Dead Things." CENTER, FAR RIGHT: Sam and Dean encounter werewolves on the road to finding and defeating the Yellow-Eyed Demon. ABOVE RIGHT: Don't mess with Dean and his gun when he's had enough and wants answers.

OPPOSITE, TOP: When Sam is possessed by the demon Meg, Dean and Bobby must find a way to exorcise her without harming Sam. OPPOSITE, BOTTOM: Dean tries to get through to Sam while the younger Winchester is possessed by the demon Meg. TOP LEFT: Dean and Sam go undercover as night security watchmen to root out a monster that can disguise itself as a human. CENTER LEFT: Dean and Sam arrive at both a literal and psychological crossroads and are about to reluctantly summon a Crossroads Demon. ABOVE LEFT: The brothers investigate the potentially deadly Croatoan virus and discover its demonic origin. TOP RIGHT: Another case, another disguise, this time as janitors to face off against the Trickster. CENTER RIGHT: Breaking and entering to search for clues is a necessary but risky part of a hunter's life. ABOVE RIGHT: The Winchesters discover the rough realities of prison when they go undercover as felons.

to deal with everyday monsters, including another shapeshifter and a sneaky trickster. It doesn't help matters that the police and FBI are on the brothers' trail for various crimes, such as credit card fraud, breaking and entering, and grave desecration, along with crimes they're not even guilty of, such as the murders committed by Shapeshifter Dean, as well as a corrupt police officer. Maybe that's why Dean is tempted to stay in a djinn-induced hallucinatory reality where he's not wanted by the FBI, Sam is a nondemonic lawyer, and Mary Winchester is still alive . . .

After Sam's possession, Bobby gives the Winchester brothers demon-warding amulets to make sure they are never susceptible again, but it doesn't protect Sam from the Yellow-Eyed Demon, who teleports him to a ghost town where he's expected to fight several other "special children" to the death. Sam believes if they all work together they can all get out alive, but some of the others give in to their fears, embrace their demonic powers, and kill each other until it's just Sam and a

soldier named Jake Talley left standing. Sam gets the upper hand, but he doesn't want to kill Jake. He tries to walk away, but Jake stabs him in the back.

Sam Winchester is dead.

Unable to accept what has happened, Dean sells his soul to a Crossroads Demon to bring Sam back to life, and he's so anxious to save his brother that he agrees to give up his soul in just one year's time. Sam gets his revenge on Jake, but not before Jake uses the Colt to open the Devil's Gate, letting hundreds of demons escape into the world. The upside is that John Winchester also escapes Hell, and he holds the Yellow-Eyed Demon down while Dean shoots Azazel dead with the Colt. John vanishes with a grateful smile, hopefully going on to a better place.

Dean and Sam have avenged their parents' deaths. They should be done fighting, but there's a demon army on the loose, and Dean only has one year left to live. The Winchesters have work to do . . .

OPPOSITE: Season 2 featured several iconic guest stars, including Tricia Helfer. TOP LEFT: The Yellow-Eyed Demon is surprised to see that Dean has gotten a hold of the Colt, the only weapon that can kill Azazel … TOP RIGHT: Dean prepares to kill the Yellow-Eyed Demon with the Colt and one of its precious silver bullets. ABOVE LEFT: Dean and Sam continue to track down the Yellow-Eyed Demon until Azazel actually comes to them … ABOVE RIGHT: Another iconic guest star from season 2—Linda Blair!

HUNTERS AND ALLIES

There are monsters everywhere; in every country, in every state, and every city. Probably in every little town and village, too. Anywhere there is human flesh to eat, human hosts to be possessed or turned into more monsters, there are supernatural creatures lurking. Not many people survive encounters with these beasts, and most of the ones that do flee or hide or wind up in mental institutions. But the rare few who don't run away? They give chase and become *hunters*.

There isn't an Internet forum where hunters congregate to share tips and post help-wanted ads, and there isn't a secret hunters telephone directory, but there is one person hunters turn to when they need help or want to network with other hunters: Bobby Singer.

Bobby Singer is a surrogate father to Sam and Dean Winchester. When he's not hunting, researching supernatural threats, answering the phone in the guise of a variety of fake federal agents, or building monster-proof panic rooms, he runs an auto salvage yard. Bobby became a hunter after he had to kill his demon-possessed wife, Karen. He was shown the ropes by Rufus Turner, whom he hunted with until "the incident" in Omaha. Even when he stays home he can't avoid hunting, occasionally getting attacked by ghosts and zombies. When his pretty neighbor asks him to fix her wood chipper, he messes things up by throwing in an okami and spraying her with monster guts. She's not interested in dating after that. "Story of my life," says Bobby.

Aside from networking through Bobby, hunters have been known to exchange horror stories over brews at Harvelle's Roadhouse. Ellen Harvelle is the owner/operator. Her husband Bill died while on a hunt with John Winchester, but she doesn't hold that against Sam and Dean. She does, however, try to keep her daughter Jo from becoming a hunter. But it's a matter of "Do as I say, not as I do," because Ellen is a top-notch hunter in her own right. After the Yellow-Eyed

OPPOSITE: Bobby Singer, Sam and Dean's most trusted ally and beloved father figure. TOP LEFT: The quirky and mulleted computer genius Ash. TOP CENTER: Tough but tender Ellen Harvelle. TOP RIGHT: Ellen's daughter, Jo Harvelle. ABOVE LEFT: Cranky but accomplished hunter Rufus Turner. ABOVE CENTER: Garth is one of the most unique hunters the Winchesters have ever encountered. ABOVE RIGHT: Sheriff Jody Mills is soft on Bobby and quickly becomes a believer in the supernatural when the hunters save her from death by her own zombified family.

Demon burns down the Roadhouse, she joins Bobby and the Winchesters at the Devil's Gate, where "special kid" Jake Talley uses his mind powers to make Ellen point her gun at her own head. She's unable to stop Jake from opening the gate and letting out hundreds of demons, but she does help Bobby close the gate again. And then, years later, she sacrifices her life to help Sam and Dean (try to) kill Lucifer.

Jo Harvelle rebels against her mother, running away from the Roadhouse to follow in her father's hunting footsteps. She's handy with knives and shotguns, but inexperienced with actual hunting, and she almost dies on her first case at the hands of a serial killer ghost. The Winchesters save her, and over time she becomes a truly kickass hunter, even teaming up with her mother on occasion. When the Horseman War arrives and turns everyone in a small town against each other, however, Jo calls Ellen a "black-eyed bitch," as she thinks her

mother's been possessed by a demon. In the battle against Lucifer, Jo is mortally wounded by Meg's Hellhound, and dies in her mother's arms.

Harvelle's Roadhouse welcomes a regular flow of hunters through its doors, but one customer—Ash—likes it there so much that he sleeps in a back room, or on the pool table. Even though he got kicked out of MIT for fighting, he's a hacker, not a fighter, so he does his hunting through his computer. He even created specialized demon-tracking software. His love of the Roadhouse is his downfall, however, as he dies inside it when it's burned down, but he just carries on in Heaven, where his personal version of the afterlife looks like Harvelle's, and his computer now tracks angels instead of demons.

Due to whatever unspeakable thing happened in the past with Bobby in Omaha, Rufus Turner is a somewhat reluctant ally, although a bottle of Johnny Walker Blue Label is always a good icebreaker. And he still turns to Bobby for help in disposing of an okami he'd killed. He later returns the favor by stealing a ring that once belonged to Fergus MacLeod (the man that became the demon Crowley), although he has to swallow it to hide it from the police, before he . . . *passes* it on to Bobby. Rufus' friendship with Bobby unexpectedly ends when Bobby becomes possessed by a monster and kills him.

Another very different hunter acquaintance of Bobby's is Garth. Monsters don't get ganked by Garth, they get "Garthed." He usually hunts alone, but he has his sock puppet, Mr. Fizzles, to keep him company. At the end of a hunt, Garth doesn't relax at a place like Harvelle's—he's literally a one-drink drunk—he'd much rather ease his weary bones in a hot tub. When he does hunt with friends, he never lets them part ways without a good hug.

Sheriff Jody Mills didn't start out wanting to be a hunter. Even after seeing her undead son eat her husband and having to shoot said son in the head, Jody doesn't actively pursue hunting. She does, however, change her opinion of Bobby, whom she used to think was nothing more than a crazy drunk. In fact, sparks fly between Jody and Bobby— while she's holding a Leviathan's decapitated head, no less. Bobby's death comes as a shock to her, but it motivates her to use her police connections to watch out for supernatural-related cases on behalf of Dean and Sam.

Frank Devereaux is not exactly a hunter. He's not exactly sane, either (by his own admission, he's bipolar with delusional ideation). But he is a very useful ally. When the Leviathan learn all of Sam and Dean's aliases, Frank provides them with new identities and coaches them on ways to keep a lower profile; he even teaches Dean how to hack into security camera feeds. Frank thinks the Leviathan are after him, too, so he leaves his house and moves around in a mobile home. But his continued research into Leviathan leader Dick Roman's activities makes him a target, and the last Sam and Dean see of him is a mobile trailer full of blood.

GORDON WALKER
FRIEND TURNED FOE

Gordon Walker became a hunter obsessed with killing vampires when his sister was turned into a bloodsucker. He thinks all vampires are evil, period. So despite the fact that Sam tells him that the vampire Lenore only feeds on animals, not humans, Gordon still captures and tortures her. He even turns his knife on Sam to tempt the pacifist vampire with human blood. Big mistake. After the Winchesters free Lenore, they leave Gordon bound to a chair for three full days.

He pays the Winchesters back by trying to kill Sam. It's not actually because he's holding a grudge against the younger Winchester, but rather because he's heard about Sam's demonic gifts and now thinks Sam is the Antichrist. Gordon becomes so focused on killing Sam that even being turned into a vampire himself doesn't distract him from what he believes to be his righteous mission. But then Sam taps into the demonic powers that Gordon so fears and uses superhuman strength to decapitate Gordon with a length of barbed wire.

THE HIERARCHY OF DEMONS

Demons are human souls that were sent to Hell and became twisted into evil spirits. The Demon Sunday School version of how it all started: God prefers humans to angels, Lucifer became jealous, and as a "Screw you" to God, he tempts a human soul and twists it into the very first demon. It's what got him locked up in his supernatural cage downstairs.

Demons mostly reside in Hell, which is a prison made of bone, flesh, blood, fear—and, yes, fire. The souls in Hell suffer agonies beyond imagination, so it's no surprise they escape to our world whenever they can. Once here, they rarely stay incorporeal, preferring instead to possess humans, which they refer to as "meat-suits." They have superhuman strength and telekinetic abilities, and they love to torture people. And they'll keep riding a meat-suit even after the body's been broken or killed.

They're not without weaknesses, however. Exorcisms expel demons from people's bodies, which is great if the body's still intact, but this just sends them back to Hell. It's ideally best to gank them with a demon-killing knife or shoot them with the Colt, although that will unfortunately kill their meat-suits as well.

When hunting demons, the best way to spot them is to look for traces of sulfur, which they tend to leave behind wherever they've been. Lightning storms and cattle mutilations are often signs of demon activity as well. They can't cross lines of salt, iron and holy water burns them, Palo Santo (Holy Wood) can

pin them down, and a Devil's Trap works as advertised—trapping them until they're exorcised or the sigil is broken. For final confirmation, saying any of God's names will make them flinch and flash their demon eyes.

WHITE-EYED DEMONS

These are the demon chiefs of staff.

LILITH was the first demon ever created. In keeping with her white eyes, her signature attack is a devastating blast of white energy. As Queen of the Crossroads, all Crossroads Demons make deals for her, which is why she ultimately holds sway over Dean Winchester's soul. She happily tosses Dean to her Hellhounds, although her celebration is somewhat dampened by the revelation that her killing blast doesn't work on Sam Winchester. Of course, that's just the impression she wanted to give Sam; in truth it was all part of the master plan for freeing Lucifer. Once she got Dean down to Hell, Alastair got him to break the first seal binding Lucifer to his cage, then Lilith sent demons all over the Earth to break sixty-four more of the seals, all while she stayed one step ahead of Sam and his quickly growing demon-ganking powers. Even though she's so evil that she snacks on babies, she loves her creator so completely that she willingly sacrifices herself, allowing Sam to kill her, knowing that as the first demon, she is the last seal binding Lucifer to his cage.

ABOVE LEFT: Lilith, Queen of the Crossroads and the final seal to set Lucifer free from his cage in Hell. TOP CENTER: The King of the Crossroads, Crowley. TOP RIGHT: Azazel, the Yellow-Eyed Demon and bane of John Winchester's existence. ABOVE CENTER: Hell's master torturer Alastair's first meat-suit is a pediatrician ... ABOVE RIGHT: While his second meat-suit is a janitor that is eventually exorcised and killed by Sam Winchester.

ALASTAIR is very old and powerful, possibly the second demon ever created. He is Hell's master torturer, and he in fact tortured both John and Dean Winchester when they were in Hell. He's also responsible for getting Dean to torture other doomed souls in Perdition, thus breaking the first of Lucifer's seals. When he comes to Earth, he causes holy statues to weep blood, and he barely flinches when Sam stabs him in the shoulder with Ruby's demon-killing knife. He's so powerful that he withstands Castiel's smiting hand, and only loses his meat-suit when Anna's Grace returns and he is destroyed in the process. Once he finds a new meat-suit, he tries to kill two reapers to break another seal, but he's thwarted by Sam and Dean and captured by Castiel. Alastair gets a taste of his own medicine, however, when he's tortured by Dean, but Uriel frees the demon, and Alastair beats his torturer almost to death before Castiel stabs him in the same shoulder with the demon-killing knife. Alastair jokes that God is on his side because Castiel missed his heart. The demon then gets the upper hand on Cass and nearly sends him back to Heaven with an Enochian spell, but Sam arrives and uses his psychic demon powers to first torture and then kill Alastair.

RED-EYED DEMONS

These are the demon deal-makers, the Crossroads Demons, who make deals for the souls that fuel Hell. They can grant humans practically any wish, making their powers on par with reality-altering angels like Zachariah. It's unknown how many Cross-roads Demons there are, but Crowley is the most powerful.

CROWLEY is Lilith's right-hand man and King of the Crossroads. As a human he was a Scottish tailor named Fergus Roderick McLeod, who sold his soul for three additional inches below the waist. As a demon, his meat-suit belonged to a moderately successful New York literary agent. He only wears tailor-made suits, prefers to drink Craig whiskey, and keeps an extremely large Hellhound as a pet. His wish-granting capabilities seem to have no limits, as demonstrated when he uses Bobby's soul to find Death and steal the Horseman's scythe. With Lilith and Alastair dead and Lucifer locked up again, Crowley crowns himself the King of Hell. To gain more souls for Hell, he enters into a temporary partnership with the angel Castiel, who double-crosses him and takes all the monster souls for himself. After Castiel returns the souls to Purgatory and is blown apart by the Leviathan, Crowley attempts to form an alliance with Leviathan leader Dick Roman, who instead rejects him. Incensed, Crowley helps the Winchesters kill Roman, then sends Dean and Castiel to Purgatory.

YELLOW-EYED DEMONS

These are the demon army generals.

AZAZEL is the only known Yellow-Eyed Demon. He is the catalyst for everything that Sam and Dean Winchester have gone through. Before they were even born, he killed their grandparents (on the Campbell side) and their father, John, whom he then resurrected in return for future access to baby Sam. Killing Mary, Sam, and Dean's mother, Azazel pushed the Winchester boys and their father into becoming hunters. Even more crucial than this, by dripping his own demon blood into baby Sam's mouth on the night of Mary's death, Azazel guaranteed the brothers' lives would never be their own. The demon continued to stoke the boys' desire to hunt by killing John Winchester (again) and causing "special child" Jake to kill Sam, which in turn caused Dean to sell his soul to a Crossroads Demon. Azazel's endgame was to raise Lucifer from hell with Sam as his vessel, but he didn't live to accomplish that, thanks to Dean and a silver bullet from the Colt.

BLACK-EYED DEMONS

These are the soldiers, the thugs, the henchmen, the minions: the masses. Most are just mindless drones that do the bidding of Azazel, Lilith, or Crowley without question. But some have very distinct personalities of their own . . .

MEG is Azazel's "daughter." Meg enters the Winchesters' lives as a potential love interest for Sam, someone to pull him away from Dean, but it isn't long before she reveals that she's a demon. The brothers manage to send her back to Hell, leaving her poor broken meat-suit to die. But you can't keep a bad demon down. Soon she's back—and possessing Sam. Dean exorcises her, but she returns again inside the body of a wannabe actress. This time she's on a mission for the Devil himself. She has to find a powerful weapon known as the Michael Sword, which turns out to be Dean. She unleashes a pack of Hellhounds on Dean, but he survives and helps Sam send Lucifer

back to his cage, which leaves Meg on the run from the new King of Hell, Crowley. The scheming demon helps Sam and Dean attack the Leviathan in order to stay close to the mentally unstable Castiel, whom she hopes to eventually use as a weapon against Crowley. Her plan backfires, and she walks right into Crowley's clutches, but flees before the demon can destroy her. However, she is soon captured and taken back to hell.

RUBY is Lilith's most loyal follower. When Ruby first jumps into the fray, rescuing Sam from the demonic incarnations of Pride, Greed, and Gluttony, she appears to be just another hunter—one who happens to have a knife that *kills* demons. But even when the Winchesters learn she's a demon, she leads them to consider whether she could actually be a *good* demon. To further earn their trust, she shows Bobby how to make new bullets that will work in the Colt, and tells Sam she wants to help him find and kill Lilith, the demon who holds the deed to Dean's soul. But she has a personal reason for wanting Lilith dead—Lilith is the demon that sent her to Hell. Ruby was once a witch, but she tells Sam she never turned evil in Hell like other souls eventually did.

Sam wants to believe her, but Dean is unconvinced—and rightly so. Despite her promises, Ruby doesn't stop Lilith from sending Dean to Hell. In fact, Lilith uses Ruby's meat-suit to get close to Dean. Despite that, Sam still trusts Ruby when she comes back, especially since she makes a point of possessing a freshly dead, soul-free body. She trains Sam to use the demonic powers Azazel gave him, eventually getting Sam to drink her blood. Once he's addicted to the power gained from her demonic blood, Sam finally kills Lilith, which appears to be a good thing, until it's revealed that Ruby has kept an important fact from him: killing Lilith breaks the final seal that frees Lucifer from Hell. But Ruby's victorious gloating is short-lived, as Sam grabs hold of her and Dean stabs her with her own demon-killing knife.

ABOVE, LEFT TO RIGHT: Meg's second meat-suit is a pretty wannabe actress who causes no end of trouble for Dean and Sam. The deceitful Ruby first appears as a petite blond with a sharp tongue. At Sam's insistence, Ruby reappears in the body of a young woman who had just been declared brain dead.

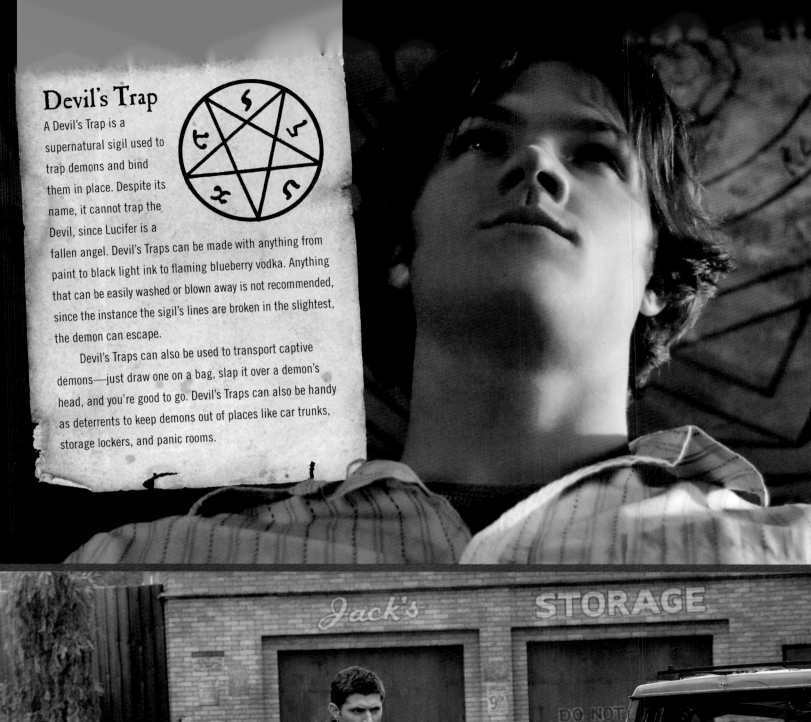

Devil's Trap

A Devil's Trap is a supernatural sigil used to trap demons and bind them in place. Despite its name, it cannot trap the Devil, since Lucifer is a fallen angel. Devil's Traps can be made with anything from paint to black light ink to flaming blueberry vodka. Anything that can be easily washed or blown away is not recommended, since the instance the sigil's lines are broken in the slightest, the demon can escape.

Devil's Traps can also be used to transport captive demons—just draw one on a bag, slap it over a demon's head, and you're good to go. Devil's Traps can also be handy as deterrents to keep demons out of places like car trunks, storage lockers, and panic rooms.

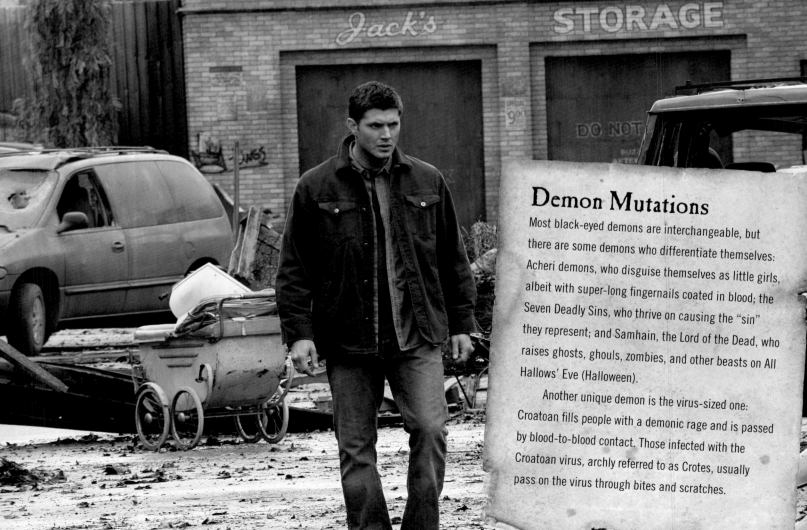

Demon Mutations

Most black-eyed demons are interchangeable, but there are some demons who differentiate themselves: Acheri demons, who disguise themselves as little girls, albeit with super-long fingernails coated in blood; the Seven Deadly Sins, who thrive on causing the "sin" they represent; and Samhain, the Lord of the Dead, who raises ghosts, ghouls, zombies, and other beasts on All Hallows' Eve (Halloween).

Another unique demon is the virus-sized one: Croatoan fills people with a demonic rage and is passed by blood-to-blood contact. Those infected with the Croatoan virus, archly referred to as Crotes, usually pass on the virus through bites and scratches.

BEHIND THE SCENES

TOP LEFT: The various stunt and filming versions of Ruby's demon-killing blade. ABOVE LEFT: Angel-killing blades all lined up in a neat and lethal row. ABOVE RIGHT: The Antichrist temporarily turns Castiel into an action figure, complete with angel blade accessory! BELOW: One of the most iconic (and coveted) props is the Colt from seasons 1, 2, and 5.

PROPS AND SET DECORATION

"For the props department, this show is simply awesome," exclaims property master Christopher Cooper. "The stuff we get to deal with, the stuff we get to create and build and play with . . . like the bottomless weapons cache hidden underneath the Winchester car's trunk floor, the Colt, the demon-killing knife, the angel-killing daggers, Castiel's action figure, etcetera. Simply awesome."

"The props department is involved in just about every shot one way or another," Cooper adds. Likewise, so is set decoration. Anything that gets used by the characters is a prop; anything that's in the background is set decoration. And set decorator George Neuman enjoys decorating the set just as much as Cooper enjoys making the props. In fact, Neuman is so proud of each set that he can't choose a favorite. "I'm happy with the final product of pretty much everything we do. A lot of

thought goes into it; when you get to that point, it's had a lot of people's fingerprints on it, so I've never walked away from the set at the end of the day going, 'Well I don't know about this. Hopefully, no one says anything . . .'"

The props also have a lot of people's fingerprints on them. "The props are designed through a collaborative effort," explains Cooper. "My department and I come up with the initial idea and then bounce it off the production designer. When we're happy with the idea, we [bring it to] the director. Then, with the help of the art department and everybody else, the prop becomes a reality. We work together, racing the clock to make it to camera."

TOP LEFT: Part of the interior of John Winchester's massive storage locker. TOP RIGHT: Jensen Ackles wields one of the hunters' rifles designed by Props. ABOVE LEFT: Another up-close view of John Winchester's storage locker. ABOVE CENTER: The Hex Box containing the magical rabbit's foot from season 3's "Bad Day at Black Rock." ABOVE RIGHT: Everything from the sheriff's badge to the fake gas lamps in season 6's "Frontierland" is carefully designed and implemented to appear authentic.

Art director John Marcynuk shares one of the ways he was involved with dressing John Winchester's storage locker in "Bad Day at Black Rock." "It was fun creating John's lockup," he says. "The wild boar skull that had the shotgun in it was originally just a shotgun in the script, but I was like, 'Well, I think he would hide it with something else just to add a little more menace.' And I love the coffin in the background—that was a George Neuman touch. Very John Winchester! Also, you don't see it, but we took the monkey from Harvelle's Roadhouse and hid it in there."

Sometimes even objects that aren't hidden don't get seen. Laments Neuman, "Sometimes, with some of the sets, you go into so much detail and they shoot a master for a few seconds, and then the rest is so tight you never really get the full scope of the set. That happens because they want the reactions of the actors rather than the background, so sometimes you only see twenty percent of the set when you watch the episode. A lot of the time you don't really see the full scope of the motel rooms; you see bits and pieces, but you don't see one big shot that

reveals the entire room." Another thing that hides the set decorations is the necessarily dark atmosphere of the episodes. For example, Neuman points out that the vampires' lair in "Dead Man's Blood" was "a huge set. We turned a barn into the lair, but because the vampires live in darkness you couldn't get the full scope of how big the place was."

On the other hand, for "Frontierland," they didn't have a problem with darkness, but rather with showing the lights on the Western set. "All the lighting back in the day was just candlelight or oil with a wick, so the challenge was to find that stuff," Neuman says. "Then we had to convert it to incandescent lighting so we could control it, and then we had to hide the lightbulb so it seemed like it's actually light from a fire or a candle."

Speaking of the Wild West, Cooper says Jensen Ackles and Jared Padalecki are "cowboys—they're competent gun-handling actors." Procuring, tinkering with, and maintaining guns for the leads and guest stars takes up a large part of the property department's time, and it's something that Cooper derives

OVERALL LENGTH 14"

TOP: The Amazon blade from season 7's "The Slice Girls," from concept art to finished prop. CENTER LEFT: Dean Winchester's standard array of hunting weapons . . . ABOVE LEFT: And his favorite gun in use. CENTER RIGHT: Sam Winchester's standard array of hunting weapons . . . ABOVE RIGHT: And his favorite gun in use.

TOP, LEFT AND RIGHT: The Hand of Glory prop from season 5's "Red Sky at Morning." ABOVE LEFT: Hex bags of various colors and sizes for various demonic and otherwise supernatural needs. ABOVE RIGHT: The hidden basement of the Goddess of Truth, Veritas, is not for the faint of heart.

great pleasure from. But there's one gun in particular that Cooper speaks of with added fondness. "Our weapons guy here in Vancouver has got a safe that's a whole floor of his building. It literally has every weapon ever made, and multiples of those. All changed to work for film. There was a gun of his that I admired for years that I thought I'd never have an opportunity for a character to use, and now it's Dean's gun."

Creator Eric Kripke has a similar story about the Hand of Glory prop. "The Hand of Glory in 'Red Sky at Morning' became a MacGuffin of the story because it's what the boys needed to find and it's what Bela ended up selling. I always wanted to put a Hand of Glory on the show," he says, "so I was glad that we were able to use it [in season 5]."

Anything the writers dream up, the crew is happy to find or make, but some things don't fit into the budget, while other things simply can't be found. Finding high-end items, for example, as they did for Veritas' apartment in "You Can't Handle the Truth," "isn't really a challenge," Neuman says. "There are definitely suppliers, but some of the stuff is too expensive." Most of the expensive items can be rented, Neuman notes, but that's also problematic. "You don't want to put a ten-thousand-dollar sofa on set and have it damaged or anything like that, so even though it would fit the scene best, you gotta go a step down sometimes. That's a challenge, but it's nothing like the challenge of finding retro stuff. You should try getting a dozen nice [matching authentic retro] diner stools . . ."

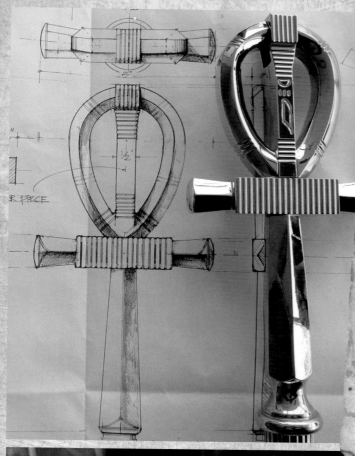

The Staff of Osiris

"The Staff of Osiris is a great piece," enthuses Christopher Cooper. "I love that thing! First, we designed it here in the art department. Then I have an incredibly talented guy who's a metallurgist and a sword maker. He's done about ninety percent of our metal props, and he builds the leather scabbards for swords and that kind of stuff, too. The staff is a combination of hand-carving and metalwork with some machined pieces. It's all screwed together and then everything was gold plated. It turned out really well. And that originally wasn't even a scripted item! It was scripted that Osiris had a gavel, but Bob Singer directed that episode, and he decided it'd be cool if Osiris had a staff that he could bang on the ground."

CHAPTER 3

THE ROAD TO HELL

SEASON 3: THE STORY

After being brought back from the dead, Sam is determined to find a way to get Dean out of his one-year deal with the Crossroads Demon, but Dean refuses to break the deal because it would result in Sam dying once again. Sam doesn't give up, however, and tries everything he can think of, including offering his soul in trade to a Crossroads Demon, whom he then ruthlessly kills for refusing the offer, and allying with the demon Ruby, who wants to kill Lilith, the demon who holds the contract to Dean's soul. He also tries to convince his brother to use the psychotic Doc Benton's scientific method for immortality, even though it would require Dean to harvest other people's organs and body parts, but Dean would rather go to Hell than turn himself into a real-life Frankenstein's monster.

While his brother searches for a way to nullify his demon deal, Dean resigns himself to the fact that he only has one year left to live. He tries to make the best of it by indulging even more than usual in junk food, alcohol, and casual sex. While investigating a changeling attack, Dean spends time with old flame Lisa Braeden and her son Ben (who happens to be a *lot* like Dean). The experience gives him a glimpse of

what life after hunting could look like, but he decides there's no point even considering a happily-ever-after when the end of his short life story's already been written. His defeatist attitude causes him to take even greater risks when fighting monsters. In fact, he purposely visits the most haunted house in America, where he encounters wannabe monster hunters Harry Spangler and Ed Zeddmore, who have surrounded themselves with like-minded amateur ghost hunters trying to shoot a reality show called *Ghostfacers*. One of the Ghostfacers doesn't survive the case, but a guilty Dean does.

A magically lucky rabbit's foot gives Dean momentary hope that touching it could counteract his demonic deal somehow, but Bobby warns him that the good luck quickly turns rotten. Everyone who touches and loses the rabbit's foot dies within a week. The problem is, Sam's already touched the rabbit's foot and lost it to master thief Bela Talbot. Dean retrieves the cursed object and burns it, but the brothers still feel cursed every time they run into Bela, who is nothing but trouble. It turns out she also has a demon deal with Lilith that is about to become due, but instead of working with the Winchesters to kill her, she

OPPOSITE: Dean prepares to face what will most likely be the last year of his life by doing what he does best—ganking monsters. TOP: When Sam tries to make a deal with a Crossroads Demon to cancel Dean's deal, she rejects his offer, and Sam responds by killing her. ABOVE LEFT: The mysterious demon Ruby says she wants to help the Winchesters defeat Lilith, but can she be trusted? ABOVE RIGHT: Sam finds himself trusting Ruby and wanting to work with her, much to Dean's dismay. LEFT: Despite the uncertainty of the coming year, Dean is never more at home than when he is behind the wheel of his beloved car.

TOP LEFT: Sam investigates pagan gods who are wreaking holiday havoc on innocent townsfolk. TOP RIGHT: Rogue hunter Gordon's back, this time as a vampire, the very creature he was dedicated to destroying. And he's out for Sam's blood. CENTER LEFT: Sam and Dean come face to face with the Ghostfacers once more ... ABOVE LEFT: Two brothers against the world, even though that world keeps getting more and more complicated—and deadly. ABOVE RIGHT: Despite the ticking clock of Dean's last year on Earth, monsters need to be hunted, so the Winchesters keep duty first. OPPOSITE, TOP: A spray-painted Devil's Trap comes in handy when Ruby needs to be kept in her place, literally. OPPOSITE, BOTTOM LEFT: Lisa Braeden's son Ben is disturbingly like a pint-sized Dean. OPPOSITE, CENTER RIGHT: Lisa Braeden, one of Dean's more memorable past flings, proves an unlikely ally when Dean investigates sightings of a changeling in the suburbs. OPPOSITE, BOTTOM RIGHT: An exasperated Sam encounters the Ghostfacers for a second time, and they are just as incompetent as ever ...

TOP LEFT: Bela Talbot wants the cursed rabbit's foot, as her client will pay her a handsome sum for it. TOP RIGHT: Before Dean can burn the troublesome rabbit's foot, Bela drops a bead on him, and she's ready to shoot to kill. CENTER LEFT: Sam decides to make Dean's last Christmas as festive as possible, complete with a real fir tree decorated with fir-scented air fresheners … CENTER RIGHT: In true Winchester fashion, the brothers exchange utilitarian gifts of beer and porn. ABOVE LEFT: Dean's last-minute research on how to get out of his deal with the Crossroads Demon takes its toll on his physical and emotional health. ABOVE RIGHT: Dean and Sam have a heart-to-heart talk before they embark on what may be their last mission together. OPPOSITE, TOP LEFT: Lilith, now in Ruby's meat-suit, summons her Hellhounds to take Dean to Hell. OPPOSITE, TOP RIGHT: Sam may not be affected by Lilith's powers, but the nasty demon makes sure he has a front-row seat for his brother's execution. OPPOSITE, BOTTOM LEFT: Dean is ripped apart by the vicious (and invisible) Hellhounds. OPPOSITE, BOTTOM RIGHT: Sam cradles his dead brother's body as he says his final good-byes.

steals the Colt from them to trade for her life. No such luck: Bela is torn to shreds by Hellhounds, and the Colt is lost.

Even though Sam's psychic premonitions disappeared after the Yellow-Eyed Demon died, Ruby is adamant he's retained his demon-given powers and keeps trying to convince him to let her teach him how to use them, since that's the only way he'll be strong enough to kill Lilith. Dean is equally adamant that Sam should not use his powers, fearful that Sam will himself be turned into a monster. It appears Ruby is right about Sam's powers, however; in a battle to the death with hunter-turned-vampire Gordon Walker, Sam uses superhuman strength to decapitate Gordon with barbed wire held in his bare hands; an incident that shocks Dean. Ruby has a special demon-killing knife that she uses freely on demons to convince the Winchesters that she's on their side. She even convinces Sam that she can help Dean get out of his crossroads deal, but

later admits to Dean that no one can. Worse yet, Dean is doomed to become a monster, since all souls that go to Hell are eventually twisted into demons. Things look more hopeless than ever, and Dean confesses to Sam that he truly doesn't want to die.

As the end of the year nears, Sam still hasn't found a way to save Dean, so the Trickster tries to get him used to the idea of Dean dying—by killing Dean over and over again, much to Sam's horror. But those "trick" deaths are nothing compared to the real thing. When the time comes, Lilith telekinetically pins Sam to a wall and makes him watch as Hellhounds tear Dean apart. Surprisingly, when Lilith tries to kill Sam, her supernaturally charged blast of white energy has no effect on him—another sure sign that demonic powers are coursing through his veins. Lilith quickly flees, but it's too late: Dean is dead.

FEMME FATALE: BELA TALBOT

"I liked the idea that Bela existed as this mercenary that just didn't give a shit about the cause," comments former executive producer Sera Gamble. "All of these supernaturally aware people that we've met are altruistic; they just want to save people because they've been touched in a horrible way by the supernatural. I thought somebody who just wants to get rich was cool."

Bela Talbot is a master thief with a special knack for communicating with ghosts who specializes in stealing and selling supernatural objects. When she steals a cursed rabbit's foot from John Winchester's storage unit, she runs afoul of Sam and Dean. The brothers both become cursed and plan to burn the rabbit's foot, but only caring about the money she'd lose, Bela shoots Sam to stop Dean from destroying it. Instead, Dean tricks her into touching the cursed trinket, forcing her finally to destroy it. She doesn't leave empty-handed, though, as she steals thousands of dollars' worth of winning lottery tickets from Dean . . .

The next time she runs into the brothers, she manipulates them into helping her steal the Hand of Glory, an occult object that can open any door, no matter how thick, well locked, or guarded. But when Sam and Dean save her from a murderous ghost, she shows her gratitude by giving them $10,000 from the sale of the Hand. Their uneasy truce holds long enough for the Winchesters to procure some dream root through her, but then she steals the Colt from them. It transpires that she made a deal with a Crossroads Demon when she was younger in exchange for having her abusive parents killed. When her contract becomes due, she tries to trade the Colt for her soul, giving it to Lilith's right-hand man, Crowley, but he keeps the Colt instead and Bela goes to Hell.

OPPOSITE: A pissed-off Bela must destroy the cursed rabbit's foot before she can claim her large finder's fee. TOP: Bela feigns a fainting spell so that she and Dean can get closer to the room containing their prize: the Hand of Glory, an object that can open any door—perfect for a big-time thief like Bela. ABOVE LEFT: Dean and Bela make unlikely partners when they find themselves roped into obtaining the Hand of Glory for a greedy client. ABOVE RIGHT: Bela comes clean to Dean about her deal with Lilith and tells him he's not the only one whose time is up …

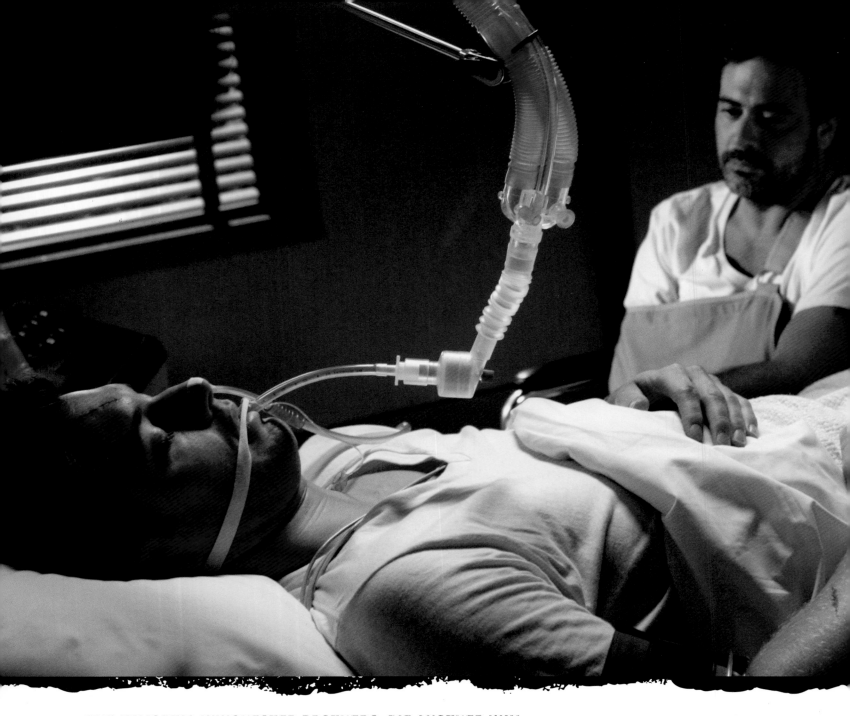

THE IMMORTAL WINCHESTER BROTHERS: DIE ANOTHER WAY

How many times have the Winchester brothers died? God only knows for sure—quite literally. When Dean and Sam wind up in Heaven after getting murdered by a misguided hunter, resident Heaven expert Ash reveals that the brothers have been there before and have had their memories wiped by angels (presumably in order to keep them alive long enough to become Michael's and Lucifer's vessels).

As far as can be determined, Dean died first. He perished shortly after being reunited with his father, John, after succumbing to injuries from a demonic big-rig hit-and-run, but he was saved by the Yellow-Eyed Demon in exchange for his father's soul. Dean died again when his Crossroads Demon deal came due, but, after decades of torment in Hell, he was resurrected by Castiel. He passed away once more when he was trying to get Sam's soul back, but died by choice so that he could talk to Death, who fortunately brought him back to life at the end of their heady conversation.

Of course, having his life and memories toyed with by an angel is nothing new for Dean; he died over a hundred different ways when he repeated the same deadly day over and over again thanks to the Archangel Gabriel (in the guise of the Trickster). As hard as those daily deaths were on his brother Sam, they were darkly humorous for *Supernatural* fans and cast and crew alike. "We sure picked some great ways to do it," notes executive producer Robert Singer on the episode titled "Mystery Spot." "I don't know that we could top what we did." Probably not, but it's fun to speculate on other entertaining ways Dean could've met his demise. "There were a lot of deaths left on the writing room floor," says story editor and current showrunner Jeremy Carver. "I think at one point I wrote free skydiving lessons, and buying a new gun . . ."

"Probably the worst way would be him dying in a car crash in his Impala," points out Jensen Ackles. "Destroying the car and himself at the same time wouldn't make him too happy." But a regular car crash wouldn't do; first assistant director Kevin Parks instead suggests, "He's working on the car and has it jacked up, and the jack falls out and he gets *squished* underneath it!" Production designer Jerry Wanek adds Sam

OPPOSITE: John Winchester watches over Dean's comatose body before deciding to make a deadly deal with Azazel, the Yellow-Eyed Demon. TOP LEFT: Dean's death at the claws of Lilith's Hellhounds is anything but pretty and painless. ABOVE RIGHT: A devastated Dean keeps vigil over Sam's lifeless body before making the deal for Sam's life with a Crossroads Demon. ABOVE LEFT: The Trickster teaches Sam a lesson about accepting Dean's fate by killing his brother over and over and over again ...

into the automobile death theme. "Maybe Dean's in the trunk and Sam's in a hurry, and Sam backs over him with the car. Just to see the look on Sam's face would be priceless."

Jared Padalecki, on the other hand, had a totally different idea: "I'd have him drowning in mud," while producer Todd Aronauer suggests, "We could have had a quick sequence of things falling on him, crushing him—different splat moments." That sequence could've ended with former visual-effects supervisor Ivan Hayden's idea: "I think a Mack truck with Dean in the foreground which actually turns him into hamburger as he gets smashed ... Jensen would've giggled like a schoolgirl after he got to see himself."

And as for Sam's demises? The rogue angel Anna initially appeared as innocent as a nun—until she impaled Sam on a broken pipe, but fortunately her work was undone by the Archangel Michael (in John Winchester's body). Although

that death occurred in 1978, chronologically speaking, it was Sam's third death. His first was one of the most shocking, gut-wrenching moments of the series. He got stabbed in the back by psychic child Jake and died in his brother's arms, only to be resurrected thanks to Dean's deal with a Crossroads Demon. Then, in a death as darkly humorous as any of Dean's in "Mystery Spot," Sam ran afoul of magically lovesick Hope Lynn Casey in "Wishful Thinking," and got incinerated by a bolt of lightning, although fortunately, her cursed wish was almost immediately reversed. Lastly—for now—Sam martyred himself by jumping into Hell with Lucifer hitchhiking in his meat-suit, only to be brought back from the depths of damnation by the tag team of Castiel and Death.

After seven seasons, the Winchester brothers live on ... to die another day.

TOP LEFT: Samuel Colt and his signature demon-killing weapon. TOP RIGHT: Dean uses the Colt and a single silver bullet to kill the Yellow-Eyed Demon. ABOVE LEFT: After Bella gave the Colt to Lilith in a desperate gamble to save her life, it wound up in the possession of the Crossroads Demon Crowley. ABOVE RIGHT: The Colt rests in its special wooden case along with the precious few silver bullets.

SPECIAL WEAPONS: THE COLT AND THE DEMON-KILLING KNIFE

In 1835, as Halley's comet lit up the sky, Samuel Colt assembled a very special gun. While its barrel is the key that unlocks the Devil's Gate he built in Wyoming, he ultimately built the weapon for hunting supernatural creatures. It has a pentagram on the handle and is engraved with Latin words that translate to "I will fear no evil." Legend says this gun can kill anything, although that's not quite true. It kills demons, vampires, and phoenixes without a problem. But it can't kill Lucifer, and the fallen archangel claims there are four other things in all of creation it can't kill—likely the other three archangels, and Death.

TOP LEFT: The Art Department's conceptual sketch for Ruby's knife, compete with demonic inscription. TOP RIGHT: The demon-killing blade in all its deadly glory. ABOVE: Ruby defensively wields her signature demon-killing knife.

Samuel Colt made thirteen numbered silver bullets for the gun, of which five remained when John Winchester came into possession of the weapon, and, with John and his sons making full use of it, the bullets soon ran out. Then along came Ruby with her special knife that kills demons as readily as the Colt. Unfortunately, it only kills demons, but it's still a wickedly sharp weapon for harming other crea-tures, and it comes in handy for chopping off Horsemen's ring fingers.

The demon-killing knife's origins are unknown, and the engravings on its blade are unknowable, but it seems likely Ruby made it herself since she had the know-how to make the Colt work again without Samuel's magic bullets, a skill she shared with Bobby Singer.

GHOSTFACERS™

LEGENDS IN THEIR OWN MINDS

ABOVE: The Hell Hounds' original incarnation included only Harry Spangler and Ed Zeddmore.

The Ghostfacers are "professional" paranormal investigators who document their ghost-hunting adventures for their homemade reality series. Ed Zeddmore and Harry Spangler are the Ghostfacer founders and team leaders, Maggie Zeddmore is the team's researcher, Spruce is the cameraman, and Corbett is their intern. According to his adopted sister, Maggie, Ed has been obsessed with the supernatural since they were kids, and when he met Harry at computer camp it was love at first geek. Before they founded Ghostfacers, Ed and Harry ran a website called Hell Hound's Lair, and their readers actually made a tulpa (a being created by thoughts) come to life. That's when *amateur* monster hunters Sam and Dean Winchester muscled in on their turf, so Ed and Harry took off for Hollywood.

But it was not to be; destiny guided them instead to Milwaukee, where they set up the official Ghostfacers headquarters in Ed's parents' garage. That's when Maggie joined them—and a romance between her and Harry blossomed. It was here that they learned that Spruce is fifteen-sixteenths Jewish and one-sixteenth Cherokee, making him a "shamanologist," and knew that fate had brought them together. The Ghostfacers' first real ghost encounter—trapped in a haunted house with the Winchester brothers and the ghosts of Freeman Daggett and his party guests—unfortunately gets Corbett killed. Corbett's ghost then gets caught in a death echo, where he reveals that he's secretly in love with Ed, so Ed is able to talk him out of the echo, then Ghost Corbett crosses over and drags Daggett with him, saving his friends.

Best of all, the Ghostfacers got it all on video! The problem is, the Winchesters don't appreciate art—they erased *everything*. But fear not: the Ghostfacers are still facing ghosts—and making self-help videos so you can hunt, too! Ed, Harry, Maggie, and Spruce, along with new intern Ambyr, continue their quest to document ghosts for the world to witness. Watch them at www.thewb.com/shows/ghostfacers.

ON SET WITH THE GHOSTFACERS

Nicholas Knight went behind the scenes to watch "Ghostfacers" being filmed, then caught up with actors Travis Wester, AJ Buckley, and Brittany Ishibashi afterward to ask them about the unique shooting experience.

NICHOLAS KNIGHT: On the set of "Ghostfacers," you went into the fully enclosed house all by yourselves, with no marks to hit and with the only cameras being the ones you wore or mounted yourselves. Was it fun to shoot the scenes like that?

TRAVIS WESTER: It was unlike any other acting experience I've ever had. I've been on stage a number of times, but that thing with the Ghostfacers was a 100 percent original experience. The

fact that when we were performing there were no camera guys, no lighting guys, no people off to the side of the camera, and no other people walking around can't be understated. It was so unreal that it became real. We were just so in the scene that it was easy to participate in the world that we were creating.

AJ BUCKLEY: It was freeing as an actor because it was a 360-degree set, so everything was live. The only thing that was hard was that when we were shooting on the day, we couldn't pan up too high [because the roof wasn't finished], which was made even harder because Jared and Jensen are giants.

TW: They're actually eleven feet tall in real life.

TOP: "Professional" ghost hunters Harry and Ed explore a haunted house for their TV show, only to run into Sam and Dean Winchester, who remain constant thorns in their sides. ABOVE: Dean is as much amused as he is annoyed at the Ghostfacers' ineptitude.

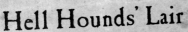

Hell Hounds' Lair

For the Ghostfacers' first appearance, as the so-called Hell Hounds in season 1's "Hell House," the producers created a real www.hellhoundslair.com website, which creator Eric Kripke had hoped would take on a life of its own. "I'd always envisioned an online presence where people discussed and traded urban legends," he explains, "and where they talk about the legend from that week's episode of *Supernatural*. I think urban legends are fascinating from a cultural place, from an academic place. Some of my favorite fan letters are from people who have been turned on to urban legends because of the show. One teacher wrote me that she used *Supernatural* as a way to teach her class a unit on urban legends and American folklore, which to me was about the highest compliment anyone ever paid us."

TOP LEFT: Ed researches their latest case on the Ghostfacers' customized laptop. TOP RIGHT: A.J. Buckley and Travis Wester are the suave and dashing leaders of the Ghostfacers! ABOVE RIGHT: Harry proudly points out the Ghostfacers' hunters' wall of research and clipped articles.

AJB: So we had to shoot them but try not to get the roof, which was next to impossible. But it was really freeing. We'd bust through six to seven pages of dialogue, and each scene would flow into the next scene. It was just cool.

BRITTANY ISHIBASHI: We had so much fun, but it was nerve-wracking. I was like, "Oh God, I hope I got something okay or they're going to fire me." But it turned out great, and it was such an honor to have that much responsibility. It was an amazing, once-in-a-lifetime experience.

NK: Would *you* go into a house that you believe is actually haunted?

BI: I wanna say yes, but . . . how haunted are we talking?

NK: As real as it gets!

BI: You know, I probably would do it just to say that I have, but it'd be terrifying, so maybe I'd change my mind.

FACE TO FACE WITH THE REAL GHOSTFACERS

With the harrowing events of the Morton House safely behind them, Ghostfacers Ed Zeddmore and Harry Spengler—with a special appearance by Maggie Zeddmore—fill us in on how the Ghostfacers came about in the first place.

NICHOLAS KNIGHT: After that incident with Mordechai Murdock's ghost in Texas, the two of you—then calling yourselves the Hell Hounds—were last seen burning rubber for Hollywood, but rumor has it that you never made it there . . .

HARRY SPENGLER: We tried to get to Hollywood; we tried our best, but it just didn't happen. We wound up having to go back home to Milwaukee. We got some jobs at Kinko's and worked our way up the system there, and eventually we got a core of people around us that were interested in the same things we were. Ghostfacers just turned out to be the next logical step.

NK: Tell us about the rest of the Ghostfacers.

ED ZEDDMORE: Spruce is the man.

HS: Um, yeah.

NK: *Oh-kay.* Um, what about Corbett? (May he rest in peace.)

EZ: Corbett was the best first intern we ever had, by far. He really took one for the team, so to speak.

HS: We mourn Corbett. I don't know if I'd say we *miss* Corbett—

EZ: Because he is always with us.

HS: His presence is felt.

EZ: We do feel him.

NK: Speaking of feelings, tell us about what happened between you and Maggie at the Morton House, Harry.

HS: I think the heightened emotions of being in that house are what revealed our true feelings.

EZ: I would prefer not to get into the Harry-Maggie discussion because it will get me going. "You can't fornicate where you eat" is my motto.

HS: That's gross.

ABOVE: Harry Spangler and Ed Zeddmore address viewers in the Ghostfacers webisode series.

ABOVE: Harry and Ed are undeterred in their quest for the unknown and unexplained, even at the cost of their own safety. Sort of.

EZ: I'm sorry, but I love Maggie. It's trendy to have an adopted sister.

NK: Here's Maggie now. Let's ask her . . .

MAGGIE ZEDDMORE: There was always something with Harry and me. We're very similar, and we respect a lot of the same things, and we're interested in a lot of the same things. My gripe with Harry is that I think he has to walk the walk a little bit more, and I think Harry's gripe with me is that I outsmart him. But we definitely have a connection. I think just being in that situation only heightened it.

NK: Maggie, tell us how you fit in with the Ghostfacers team.

MZ: I'd say I'm definitely an overachiever. I want to know why—I want to know what ghosts are and why they appear. I'm like the Scully of the operation. I can't deny what I'm seeing, but at the same time I know that there has to be some sort of an explanation.

NK: Okay, so how do you go about finding real ghosts to study in the first place?

EZ: We're just a couple of squirrels trying to get some nuts.

HS: That's a good way to put it, Ed. That's a very good way to put it.

EZ: Not like those little squirrels. We're big and furry, with bushy tails.

HS: Healthy looking.

EZ: Healthy-looking squirrels trying to get some big ol' nuts.

NK: If there are other people interested in the same nutty things as you are, how can they contact you?

EZ: The world needs more 'Facers. If you want to join the movement, contact us at www.ghostfacers.com.

HS: Stay razor!

ABOVE, LEFT AND RIGHT: Production designer Jerry Wanek and late director Kim Manners scout locations for the season 3 episode "No Rest for the Wicked."

THE ART DEPARTMENT—PRODUCTION DESIGN

When production designer Jerry Wanek joined *Supernatural* (starting with the first episode filmed in Vancouver, season 1's "Wendigo"), he brought along a fully assembled team of talented artists. Coming off genre shows like *John Doe* and *Dark Angel*, they hit the ground running on *Supernatural*. "My crew and I had done a few other shows that had these sorts of textures," elaborates Wanek. "We had a lot of practice with dark and moody from doing *Dark Angel* because that was post-apocalyptic, so we had a pretty good idea as to what worked and what didn't work as far as the palette and direction we should go in. Even though it was a totally different show, they still had a lot of the same tonal qualities."

For the most part, *Supernatural* has kept those dark and moody tones, but a challenge Wanek's team faced in season 4 was how to match the modern *Supernatural* feel when filming an old-style, black-and-white monster movie. "Oddly enough, we still picked colors," says art director John Marcynuk. "We did a test on a color sheet while shooting in black-and-white with our digital camera to see what kind of contrast we would get, and that enabled us to pick the best colors to use. It was really fun shooting in black-and-white."

"We had to build a stereotypical dungeon for 'Monster Movie,'" Wanek reminisces, "and it was a lot of fun. *Supernatural* just gives us such a wide variety of stuff to draw from. For example, I loved the replica dollhouse that we had to build to match the mansion in 'Playthings.' I was amazed by what the construction crew did, and the set dec guys, and everyone that worked on it. As it turns out, a couple of guys on the crew build miniatures as a hobby, so we were able to build it for a little more than half of what it would have cost [from an outsourced dollhouse maker] and with twice the detail. I just thought the results were incredible. Also, when you're doing things [with outside contractors], there's no way to monitor the process, so if something changes in the script or we need to make an adjustment, that's a really tough thing to do. This way, we were able to keep on top of it, and the results were stunning."

But the dollhouse wasn't just a visually captivating piece of the production design for that episode; it served a very important, very creepy purpose in the story. "I don't care if it's a motel room or if it's the hunters' compound or whatever, we don't put stuff in there for the sake of putting it in there because it looks cool," says Wanek. "I think that's really a

TOP LEFT: The Mummy (Geoff Redknap) rises from his Hollywood studio-rented crypt … TOP RIGHT: "Dracula" (Todd Stashwick) prepares to bite his next victim, a lederhosen-clad Dean. ABOVE LEFT: The laboratory set is a perfect replica of old horror-film locations, complete with operating tables and archaic controls. ABOVE RIGHT: The changeling Dracula welcomes his captive "bride" (Melinda Sward) to their bedchambers.

mistake in design. You don't want to take people out of the story. It's really a challenge to not only have something that looks cool, that's very graphic, but that also makes sense to the place we're in. There's a lot of thought that goes into that, and there are a lot of things that are rejected even though they sound cool, because the first thing we have to do is service the story." Considering the number of motels, diners, old houses, and warehouses that they regularly create on *Supernatural*, Wanek adds, "for us it's always a challenge to try to bring something fresh to the designs."

As such, while they could have gone with an abandoned house for the Campbell compound in season 6, Jerry and his team made a point of finding a unique location. "We knew it had to be laid out so it would be very functional as a place where hunters could gather and have their weapons," Wanek says. "Barns are always great, warehouses are great, but we've done that, so we decided that we were going to do a Quonset hut. We can easily build the interior of a Quonset hut on stage, but we had to find a matching exterior as an establishing shot, and we happened to luck out—we found a great old Quonset hut on this farm outside of town. We went from there and modeled the inside to match. We got some great

textures; there are concrete foundations walls, some great metal rounded roof panels, and it was great for lighting through because we had some corrugated plastic that would work both as diffusion and as a light source. At this farm where the Quonset hut is, we found these old cow stanchions for milking cows, so we used those as handrails inside the Campbell compound."

Similarly, after using a barn for *Supernatural's* first vampire nest in season 1's "Dead Man's Blood," when they needed to create a vampire's lair for season 6's "Live Free or Twi-hard," they eschewed the regular barns and warehouses, instead going with an old bank building. "We really amped up the creep factor from just being in some normal building to something that had a lot of character to it," notes Wanek with pride. "Whenever we have an opportunity to step outside the box a little bit, it's more fun for the production-design element. That doesn't mean that we do that every episode, because some of the scarier things that we have are when everything goes really bad in a really nice neighborhood. Those episodes where we just have to play it straight, but there's something amiss, and it's sort of like the monster next door, also plays very well into our genre.

TOP: The creepy dolls from the season 2 episode "Playthings" provide eerie company for actor Jensen Ackles. LEFT: A hunter family portrait of Sam, Dean, and their grandfather, Samuel Campbell (Mitch Pileggi), in the Campbell compound. ABOVE: Samuel Campbell is up to shady business in his office at the Campbell compound …

OPPOSITE, TOP: One of the most familiar and best-loved sets was Bobby Singer's house, full of hunting books and lore. OPPOSITE, CENTER: The Campbell compound library is well stocked and comes in handy for Sam and Dean when Bobby's impressive library comes up short. OPPOSITE, BOTTOM: A tense confrontation between grandfather and grandsons at the Campbell compound. TOP, LEFT AND RIGHT: Views of the impressive movie set built for the fictional Hell Hazers 2. ABOVE LEFT: Dean finds himself in food paradise at the set's craft-services table. ABOVE RIGHT: The Winchesters are stunned to find themselves on the surreal and haunted set of Hell Hazers 2 ...

"Every time we get a script, whether it's a motel room, a warehouse, a farmhouse, or whatever, we try to stretch it as far as we can with the money we have and the time we have to make it believable and make it creepy."

One way to save time and money is to reuse studio sets that haven't been torn down yet. For instance, according to Marcynuk, "the wonderful, tasteful apartment we created for the young woman in 'Heart' is a significant reworking of our loft set from 'No Exit,' and I think it helped establish her character."

Set design and location regularly aid in establishing characters, but sometimes even the resourceful *Supernatural* crew can't do that in the way the script calls for. Such was the case with the introduction of Eve, the Mother of All Monsters.

"It was originally supposed to be the Mother of All coming out of a lake," explains executive producer Phil Sgriccia, who directed Eve's debut episode, "Like a Virgin." "It was November and I was like, 'Hey guys, we can't!' I was frantically calling the writers for help, saying, 'We gotta think of another idea because to put a young lady in a white dress in a lake that she's supposed to float up out of in November, you're talking major money and

major time. We just don't have that kind of access and budget.'" Instead, they went with a cave, which fit perfectly with the episode's dragon motif. "We actually spent three days looking for caves," Sgriccia reveals, "then we ended up having the art department build the whole façade."

Producing a warm lake in November was one of the very rare occasions where the production team was unable to find or fabricate a suitable location. They've done practically every nook and cranny in the United States, and they've even done a cemetery in Scotland, all in and around Vancouver. For "Hollywood Babylon" they considered shooting in Hollywood itself, but even then they concluded there was no need to leave Vancouver. "We made a scouting trip down to LA to shoot this episode on a back lot," reveals Wanek. "But with budgetary concerns and time concerns and actor availability and all the other things that come into play, we realized it wasn't going to happen. Then it was up to us to turn the absence of a back lot into a back lot. Viewing the end result, I think nobody would have said, 'Oh, this is just around the corner in Vancouver.' Whenever we can fool people to that extent, that makes us feel good."

CHAPTER 4

HEAVEN AND HELL

SEASON 4: THE STORY

After four months in Hell that felt like four decades, Dean suddenly finds himself back on Earth, buried in a coffin. Digging himself out, he heads to a convenience store, where he's assaulted by a painfully high-pitched noise that shatters all the store's windows. Finding a pay phone, he tries to call for help, but Sam's number is disconnected and, worse still, Bobby hangs up on him, thinking he's a prank caller. Frustrated, Dean goes to Bobby's house, but Bobby assumes he's a monster and tries to kill him. After Dean proves he's not a demon, zombie, or any other kind of monster (despite the odd handprint burned into his left forearm), they seek out Sam in the same town Dean was buried in. Dean and Bobby both come to the conclusion that Sam must have made some dark deal to bring Dean back from damnation.

From the very moment Dean died and was cast into Hell, Sam tried everything he could think of to save his brother from eternal suffering. Initially, he attempted to open the Devil's Gate again, knowing that was how their father managed

to escape Hell, but found he couldn't do it without the supernatural powers of the Colt. When that failed, he tried bargaining with a Crossroads Demon, offering his own life in trade for Dean's, only to discover that the creature was unwilling to part with his sibling's soul. All the while, Sam had to live with the crushing guilt of knowing that it was *he* who was supposed to have died, not his older brother. Dean was rotting in Hell and there seemed to be nothing he could do to save him. Distraught and desperate, Sam succumbed to temptation and allowed the newly returned demon Ruby to teach him how to use his psychic powers. Sam is overjoyed when Dean mysteriously returns, fully human and with seemingly no memories of his time in Hell. However, fearing his brother's reaction, he keeps his psychic activities and alliance with Ruby a secret.

The trio enlists the aid of Bobby's friend Pamela Barnes, who uses her formidable psychic powers to look upon the face of the supernatural entity that raised Dean from Hell, but the

OPPOSITE: When Dean is mysteriously raised from the dead, the hunters enlist the help of psychic Pamela Barnes to help find out how. TOP: Pamela succeeds in contacting Castiel, but who or what is he? ABOVE LEFT: Pamela's contact with Castiel comes at a heavy price when her eyes are literally burned out. ABOVE: Sam's psychic powers are getting stronger, as he is now able to fully exorcise demons from their meat-suits. LEFT: Ruby's back in a new body—and she's helping Sam improve his powers. But to what end?

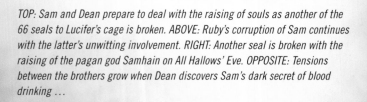

TOP: Sam and Dean prepare to deal with the raising of souls as another of the 66 seals to Lucifer's cage is broken. ABOVE: Ruby's corruption of Sam continues with the latter's unwitting involvement. RIGHT: Another seal is broken with the raising of the pagan god Samhain on All Hallows' Eve. OPPOSITE: Tensions between the brothers grow when Dean discovers Sam's dark secret of blood drinking …

sight of the creature's true visage literally burns her eyes out. With Bobby's help, Dean manages to summon the creature that raised him from Hell, who appears in the body of a man. After what happened to Pamela, Dean and Bobby are predisposed to kill first and ask questions later, but none of their weapons work. They are soon told the reason why—they are dealing with an angel named Castiel. Castiel reveals that he pulled Dean from Perdition on God's command, and that God has work for the elder Winchester brother.

Castiel also reveals that Lilith, the demon who held the lease on Dean's soul, is breaking the 66 seals that bind fallen Archangel Lucifer—aka the Devil—to his cage in Hell. The angels believe Dean is somehow the key to stopping Lucifer, but Sam thinks he's the only one strong enough to stop Lilith,

so he secretly continues practicing his demon-exorcising powers. Suspicious, Dean catches Sam in the act and reacts violently. Understanding Dean's fear that he'll turn into an evil freak, Sam promises to stop using his powers. Unfortunately, he soon encounters the demon Samhain, who creates zombies en masse and possesses much greater powers than a regular demon. Desperate to stop Samhain, Sam exorcises the demon with his mind, much to Dean's dismay. On top of that, Sam confesses to his brother that he and Ruby are lovers, although he keeps an even bigger final secret to himself. In return, Dean admits that he remembers everything that happened in Hell, and that after being tortured for what felt like thirty years, he himself then became one of Hell's torturers for another whole decade.

Haunted by his memories of Hell, Dean soldiers on. Even while hunting Lilith, Dean and Sam manage to rid the world of a slew of ghosts, demons, witches, and shapeshifters, as well as a genetically doomed rougarou and a siren that pits the brothers against each other. Shockingly, the brothers also come up against a ghoul disguised as the half-brother they never knew they had, a young man named Adam Milligan, who sadly is already dead. They encounter more angels as well, including the human-hating Uriel, who turns out to be an angel-killing Lucifer supporter, and Anna, who had chosen to become human and makes love to Dean before regaining her Grace, becoming an angel again just in time to kill Uriel. Despite everything they've been through, nothing could have prepared the Winchesters for meeting the prophet Chuck Shurley, who knows everything about them. *Everything*. But what's truly disturbing is that he's turned their real-life monster-hunting adventures into poorly selling novels, which Castiel forecasts will someday come to be known as the Winchester Gospels.

Fighting monsters is always life-threatening, but Dean comes even closer than usual to dying again when he's afflicted with a ghost sickness, and Sam *does* die (briefly) when he's

struck by lightning. Sadly, it's Pamela who dies for real when she's murdered by a demon while helping the brothers astrally project their spirits to save the reaper Tessa from the demon Alastair. Her death is not in vain, however—the Winchesters stop Alastair from breaking a seal, and Castiel captures the demon. In order to discover who is murdering dozens of Heaven's angels, Dean is forced to torture Alastair, the very demon who tormented him in Hell and taught him how to torture. Thanks to the traitorous angel Uriel, Alastair escapes the Devil's Trap he is contained in, nearly beating Dean to death before attempting to send Castiel back to Heaven. Using his psychic powers, Sam restrains the demon, then kills him.

Against Dean's wishes, and despite the angels' threats to smite him if he goes too far along his dark path, Sam has continued to strengthen his powers. Now that he's strong enough to kill demons with his mind, he's ready to fight Lilith. However, the big secret that he's been keeping is the fact that he's been drinking Ruby's blood to make him more powerful; but Ruby's gone missing, so Sam drinks the blood of another demon that he then kills. Horrified, Dean locks his brother up in Bobby's panic room, forcing him to detox

OPPOSITE: Dean and Sam meet their unknown half-brother Adam. Or rather, the ghoul that ate Adam and took his form... TOP LEFT: Jensen Ackles and Jared Padalecki show off their respective high school staff disguises in the episode "After School Special." TOP RIGHT: Brock Kelly and Colin Ford play the young Dean and Sam Winchester in the season 4 episode, "After School Special." ABOVE LEFT: Sam easily bonds with their half-brother Adam, but Dean remains characteristically suspicious. ABOVE RIGHT: The ghoul out for revenge disguised as Adam Winchester.

TOP: Sam and Dean are shocked to confront Alastair in his new meat-suit. ABOVE LEFT: Hell's master torturer, Alastair, is on Earth to kill angels and help bring about the Apocalypse… ABOVE RIGHT: Alastair's back in a new meat-suit and determined to break another of the 66 Seals. RIGHT: Once responsible for training Dean in the ways of torture, Alastair now finds himself on the opposite end of the deal.

TOP LEFT: Dean's ministrations are anything but tender as Alastair is tortured for information the angels desperately need. TOP RIGHT: When Dean is subdued by Alastair, Castiel arrives to help. CENTER LEFT: Freed from the Devil's Trap that held him captive, Alastair is out for revenge. CENTER RIGHT: Castiel tries to remove Alastair from his meat-suit, but finds his powers ineffective. ABOVE LEFT: Sam shocks both Castiel and Alastair with his rapidly growing dark powers. ABOVE CENTER: Castiel is almost no match for Alastair's demonic powers … ABOVE RIGHT: Castiel examines the broken Devil's Trap that freed Alastair.

OPPOSITE, TOP: Ruby leads Sam into her final trap in order to free the Devil … OPPOSITE, BOTTOM: Sam pins Lilith to an altar with his now fully developed special powers, but she seems almost too willing to die. LEFT: Zachariah tempts Dean with his favorite foods in order to stay in the "Beautiful Room" and let Sam kick-start the Apocalypse elsewhere. BELOW LEFT: Lilith's death is the last of the 66 Seals to be broken, and with her demise comes Lucifer's liberation from Hell… BELOW: Dean arrives too late to stop Sam from killing Lilith and starting the Apocalypse.

from his demon-blood addiction before he fully crosses over to the dark side and becomes a demon—or worse …

But the angels have their own agenda. Castiel frees Sam, allowing him to find and kill Lilith, and then Sam meets up with Ruby and drinks her blood. Dean shows up and tries to kill Ruby, but his wayward brother stops him. More than ever, Sam believes he's the only one strong enough to stop Lilith and save the world from Armageddon, so from his skewed perspective the ends justify the means. The siblings fight and Sam nearly kills Dean before leaving with Ruby, ignoring Dean's warning that if he leaves he can never come back. Dean is ready to give up on Sam, but Bobby convinces him that his brother needs him now more than ever.

Dean races after Sam, but is held up by the angel Zachariah, who reveals that the angels now *want* Lucifer to rise so that the Archangel Michael can kill him, never mind the fact that "truckloads" of humans will die in an all-out battle between Heaven and Hell. Surprisingly, Castiel decides to protect the world he has come to admire from his fellow angels, helping Dean to escape and track Sam down. Ruby, however, shuts Dean out. Fortunately (or so it seems), with just one seal left to break, Sam kills Lilith. But before he can celebrate, Ruby reveals that she's been playing him the whole time, and in killing Lilith, Sam himself has actually broken the *final* seal on Lucifer's cage. Devastated, he helps Dean kill Ruby, but it's a small consolation, because *Lucifer is rising …*

OPPOSITE: Castiel is an angel of the Lord, but his relationship with the Winchesters will eventually see him rebel from the strict rules of Heaven. TOP LEFT: Castiel makes his first majestic appearance to an awestruck Dean Winchester. TOP RIGHT: Devout Jimmy Novak became the vessel for the angel Castiel. ABOVE LEFT: Worried that Castiel is becoming too affected by his interactions with the Winchesters, the angel Uriel is assigned to keep an eye on his heavenly brother. ABOVE RIGHT: Castiel's grand plan to open the gate to Purgatory to increase his own power and raise an army to conquer Heaven is about to come to fruition, but is there more awaiting him than anticipated?

AN ANGEL NAMED CASTIEL

Angel. Soldier of God. Defender of humans. Castiel is all these things and more, and from his very first appearance, he has established himself as one of the most powerful and intriguing figures to enter the Winchesters' lives. His powers are vast, proven from the beginning when he pulled Dean out of the very depths of Hell to once again walk the Earth and fulfill his mission to stop the impending Apocalypse. He can also travel to the past, become invisible to humans, incinerate monsters, and smite demons with a simple touch. In the Winchesters' fight against evil, Castiel is an invaluable ally.

But he is not without his flaws. His bond with Dean and his affection for humans makes him weak in the eyes of other angels, and eventually his devastation at being unable to find the missing God leads him to form an unholy alliance with the Crossroads Demon, Crowley. While these all have consequences that affect both him and those around him, Castiel touchingly proves himself a little bit human along the way. Until he declares himself the new God, however, and destroys anyone—and anything—that stands in his way.

His newfound status, however, comes at a price: in addition to absorbing all the souls from Purgatory to form a new angelic army loyal only to him, Castiel absorbs the ancient and incredibly evil creatures known as Leviathan as well. As old as time and mentioned in the Bible, the Leviathan pose a threat potentially greater than the averted Apocalypse. Before he can atone for his sins, Castiel implodes, unable to hold back the Leviathan, freeing them to roam the planet. He emerges months later a changed angel, one who cannot remember his past.

Dean turns to Castiel for help in restoring Sam's fractured mind. In the process, Castiel remembers who and what he is, and the guilt that accompanies this revelation. In an effort to atone for his past sins, Castiel restores Sam's psyche and takes on the mental struggle with Lucifer himself. Now he's an unreliable player in the war against the Leviathan, and Castiel's quest to right his wrongs will be a uniquely challenging one. Helping the Winchesters kill the Leviathan leader Dick Roman is a big step in the right direction, but will Castiel have the power to help, or to hinder?

TOP: Castiel gives Sam and Dean a vial of his blood in order to help defeat the Leviathan. ABOVE: Castiel helps the Winchester brothers prepare to fight Dick Roman and the Leviathan.

MISHA COLLINS

After four seasons, Misha Collins can attest that appearing on the show has had a profound effect on him. "*Supernatural* definitely has changed my life. I have fans and stuff like that, which I never had before. As an actor, one of the questions you ask yourself is, 'How am I going to handle it when I start to get recognized? Is it going to go to my head?' But it remarkably feels much more ordinary than you would imagine. It's a change, but it's not a dramatic change—it's just something that you take into your life and keep going. I've also been inspired by the devotion of this fan base. They're just so completely involved and do some really cool stuff with that energy.

"*Supernatural* is a great set to work on. Jared and Jensen are great guys and really good friends. There's a constant background level of hazing and verbal abuse that goes on, but it's all in really good fun, and everybody here works their asses off and loves their jobs; it's a really nice environment to be in. I love the cast and the crew and the fans, and I'm really happy to be involved in the show."

"My favorite episode has been 'The French Mistake,'" Collins says. "I just think that that was five kinds of brilliant and brave at the same time. For the writers and producers to green-light that was totally awesome, and it just worked really, really well. It was so much fun to do. I tried to make the character of 'Misha the actor' as douchebag-actor-y as possible, so at every turn in the shooting I would look for a way to tweak him a little bit, make him a little bit more annoying or self-absorbed. And when that episode aired everyone was like, 'Oh, Misha, it was so awesome just to see you playing *yourself* finally.'"

A GUIDE TO ANGELS

"The angel mythology really expanded and improved on the show, but we were not sure when we introduced them whether the angel storyline was going to work," admits creator Eric Kripke. "If we'd cast the wrong person in the Castiel role, it might not have worked. We might have tried it and abandoned it! I really give Misha Collins the lion's share of the credit for saving the angel mythology."

Angels are warriors of God. They are colossal, winged beings that are multidimensional wavelengths of celestial intent. Their true forms will burn human eyes out, and their true voices will shatter glass and burst human eardrums, so they communicate via electronics (like TVs and radios) when necessary, but they will usually take on a human host. In other words, they possess people like demons do, the main difference being that they need to ask their vessel's permission. Angels can see demons' true faces, and are only too happy to smite them immediately.

Devoid of free will and human emotions, they'll follow their orders blindly, even if that means killing other angels, eradicating thousands of humans, or actually helping fallen Archangel Lucifer start the Apocalypse.

Angels can teleport at will, knock a human out cold with a touch, and enter a person's dreams. They can even travel through time, but the act takes an enormous physical toll on them. Although awe inspiring, they do have some weaknesses; a circle of Holy Fire will trap them, and both Holy Fire and heavenly weapons (such as Lot's Salt Rock) can destroy their human vessels. Plus, there are three things that can kill them: a Leviathan, one of their own angel blades, and the archangels.

There are just four archangels—Michael, Lucifer, Raphael, and Gabriel—and they are God's most terrifying warriors, able to obliterate a "regular" angel with a simple snap of their fingers.

TOP ROW: The fallen angel Anna regains her Grace, but is soon the target of sinister forces from Hell—and Heaven; The angel Balthazar is first an annoyance and then an ally to the Winchesters; tired of the war between his heavenly brothers, the Archangel Gabriel assumes the guise of the Trickster. BOTTOM ROW: Castiel is reunited with Hester, an angel from his former garrison in Heaven; Joshua is keeper of Heaven's gardens who offers Sam and Dean invaluable advice.

ANGELS FROM A TO Z

ANNA was Castiel's superior in Heaven, but she ripped out her Grace and fell to Earth so that she could experience love and chocolate. But when Dean Winchester breaks the first seal on Lucifer's cage and angels arrive on Earth to stop the breaking of more seals, the now-human Anna starts hearing angels broadcasting messages. Anna wants to remain human, but with demons trying to use her to spy on the angels and angels trying to kill her for removing her Grace, she has no choice but to reinsert it. She goes on the run, but returns to save Castiel from the rogue angel Uriel. Castiel, ever the good soldier, still sends Anna to prison in Heaven, but she eventually escapes and travels back in time to try to kill John and Mary Winchester before they can give birth to Sam, Lucifer's vessel. Ironically, Anna gets a younger Uriel to help her, but then the Archangel Michael possesses John and smites her.

BALTHAZAR once fought alongside Castiel, but thanks to the example Castiel set in tearing up the angels' rule book, he believes it's a new era with no rules and no destiny, just utter and complete freedom. As a result, he steals some heavenly weapons (such as the Staff of Moses) and fakes his own death in order to live on Earth. But he's still an ally of

sorts, turning Raphael's meat-suit to salt to save Castiel, and preventing the *Titanic* from sinking at Castiel's request. But when he discovers Castiel is working with the demon Crowley, he spies on his friend for the Winchesters, and pays for his betrayal when he's literally stabbed in the back by Castiel.

GABRIEL is the archangel formerly known as the Trickster. He disguised himself as the pagan god Loki in order to hide from his squabbling brothers, Michael and Lucifer, but he nonetheless takes a special interest in the human brothers destined to become Michael and Lucifer's vessels, Dean and Sam Winchester. His relationship with the Winchesters eventually causes him to take a s the side of humans and battles Lucifer, dying valiantly.

HESTER is a member of Castiel's former angel garrison in Heaven. Believing Castiel to be dead, she arrives on Earth to protect the new Prophet of the Lord, Kevin Tran, from harm. She is shocked to learn that Castiel is alive, but Hester is eventually killed by Meg when she tries to kill Castiel.

JOSHUA is Heaven's gardener. Even as most angels are starting to feel like God has left the building, Joshua claims to have conversations with God, though they're mostly one way. When the brothers are trapped in Heaven, he saves Sam and

Dean from Zachariah in order to deliver a message to them from God Himself.

MICHAEL is the oldest and most powerful archangel. He wants Lucifer to rise from Hell so that they can have an apocalyptic grudge match. But Castiel interrupts his plans when he destroys his eventual human vessel (Adam Milligan) with Holy Fire, before Sam Winchester yanks Michael down into Lucifer's cage in Hell, where the two angels still wrestle in a never-ending battle.

RACHEL is Castiel's lieutenant until she gets wind of his dealings with Crowley and tries to kill him, only to lose her own life to Castiel's angel blade.

RAPHAEL is a staunch supporter of his archangel brother Michael. He claims to have a better imagination than Zachariah, he protects prophets (such as Chuck Shurley), and after the first seal is broken, he does everything he can to bring on the Apocalypse so that Michael and Lucifer can end their eons-old spat once and for all. He won't let anything stop him, not even Castiel, whom he kills, and then continues to war with, in his resurrected form, despite the fact that Castiel was seemingly brought back to life by God Himself. But when Castiel takes on God-like powers of his own thanks to the souls from Purgatory, Raphael is simply wiped out of existence by a snap of the now-powerful angel's fingers.

URIEL is an angel purification specialist who feels that dealing with human "mud monkeys" is a waste of his time. He claims he can turn humans to dust just by uttering one word, but he is kept in line by Castiel. But while pretending to help Castiel stop Lilith from breaking the seals that bind Lucifer, Uriel secretly plots to break seals and kills any angels that refuse to help him free Lucifer. He fails to convert Castiel to his cause and plans to make him his next victim, but Anna kills Uriel first.

VIRGIL is an angel assassin that Raphael sends to retrieve the heavenly weapons from Balthazar, but the crafty rogue angel whips up a spell that sends Virgil chasing after the Winchester brothers to an alternate universe . . . where Virgil remains trapped to this day.

ZACHARIAH is part of Heaven's upper management. He was consistently employee of the month in Heaven before his failure to recruit Sam and Dean Winchester as vessels for Lucifer and Michael made him a laughingstock. But it wasn't for lack of trying—he gave Dean stomach cancer, then sent him to a future where Lucifer killed him, broke Sam's legs and removed his lungs, altered the brothers' reality, and used an evil illusion of their mother to psychologically torture them.

Zachariah thinks his luck's finally changed when Dean agrees to become Michael's vessel, only to discover it was a ruse for Dean to get close enough to kill him with an angel blade.

TOP ROW: Michael in the body of a young John Winchester; the deadly Virgil follows Sam and Dean into an alternate reality in order to kill them. BOTTOM ROW: Uriel proves himself a traitor to Heaven and wants to help bring about the Apocalypse; Raphael's second vessel, while softer in appearance, is no less deadly; the arrogant angel Zachariah wants to jump-start the Apocalypse and will do anything to succeed in his mission.

ABOVE: After abandoning her angelic powers, Anna reluctantly reinstates her Grace in order to help prevent the Apocalypse. OPPOSITE, TOP: The Archangel Gabriel disguised himself as the Trickster for many years before revealing his true identity. OPPOSITE, BOTTOM: Sam and Dean first meet the Trickster when he was disguised as a maintenance man in season 2's "Tall Tales."

ENOCHIAN

Enochian is the language of angels, which they use to communicate with one another in Heaven and on Earth. The language is also used in spells that involve angels, whether summoning, binding, or expelling them. There is an Enochian chant that can forcibly expel an angel from its human vessel and send it back to Heaven, and the Whore of Babylon also used one to harm Castiel when he tried to stop her plans.

Enochian sigils are glyphs of immense power used to bind demons, protect individuals from angelic detection, and prevent angels from entering or discovering spaces such as houses, rooms, or great swaths of land.

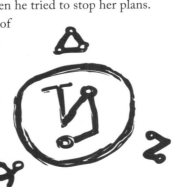

RICHARD SPEIGHT, JR.

As the Trickster, actor Richard Speight, Jr. became one of the most popular recurring characters on *Supernatural* from his first appearance in "Tall Tales," but the trick was on him, because his character wasn't who he thought he actually was. Richard was thrilled, however, to discover that the Trickster is actually the Archangel Gabriel. "At first I'd just been the guy who came in, had fun, snapped his fingers, and left," he relates. "So to realize in 'Changing Channels' that I suddenly had a significant role in the grander scheme of the mythology was awesome. I called Jeremy Carver, the episode's writer, to get information on the character and some backstory on the archangels. My episodes in seasons 2 and 3 were great, but doing episodes that matter to the overall plotline has made my experience on *Supernatural* that much better."

THE 66 SEALS

What are they? Locks on the door of Lucifer's Cage.

How many are there? 600

How do they work? Break 66 and Lucifer is freed from Hell.

Is there a combination? The first and last are crucial, but the middle 64 can be any of the other 598 . . .

The First Seal: The first seal is broken when a righteous man—in this case Dean Winchester—sheds blood in Hell.

Other Known Seals:

- Rise of the Witnesses—ghosts of people hunters failed to save from monsters.
- Samhain rises.
- Ten species go extinct in Key West.
- A fishing crew of fifteen stricken blind in Alaska.
- A schoolteacher in New York kills sixty-six children.
- Two reapers die on the night of the solstice (this seal remained unbroken).

The Final Seal: Lilith dies. As it is written, "The first demon will be the last seal."

ABOVE: The Winchesters prepare to face countless Witnesses, as one of the 66 Seals is broken. INSET: All the Witnesses bear a distinctive mark on their inner wrists, which allows Sam and Dean to deduce what they are before it's too late. OPPOSITE, TOP LEFT: The Summoning of Spirits is one of the 66 Seals that will break Lucifer out of Hell, so the reappearance of the woman the demon Meg possessed is particularly ominous. OPPOSITE, TOP RIGHT: Samhain is raised on Halloween, thereby breaking another of the 66 Seals . . . OPPOSITE, BOTTOM: Eric Kripke directs Jensen Ackles, Jared Padalecki, and Genevieve Cortese Padalecki in the final scene of the season 4 finale, "Lucifer Rising."

CHUCK SHURLEY: PROPHET OF THE LORD

Chuck Shurley is a struggling novelist who, under the pen name Carver Edlund, writes the *Supernatural* series about monster-hunting brothers Sam and Dean Winchester. A small press publisher run by Sera Siege published twenty-four books, but they didn't sell well, so *No Rest for the Wicked* became the last published title. However, Chuck continues to write the *Supernatural* series until he completes one final book, appropriately titled *Swan Song*.

Chuck uses aspirin and alcohol to help his writing process, and rather than brainstorming in the regular daydreaming fashion, he blacks out and has vivid visions of his characters' lives. Despite the fact that the books seem to be writing themselves, he is unwilling to believe that his characters are real when Sam and Dean pay him a visit. That is, until they tell him their last name, something no one could possibly know, since it's a detail he quirkily left out of all the *Supernatural* books. At first he thinks he must be a god—a cruel and capricious one, for all he's put the Winchesters through—but then the angel Castiel explains that Chuck is actually a Prophet of the Lord, and that, after the Apocalypse, his books will forever be known as the Winchester Gospels.

When Sam gets in a tight spot with the demon Lilith, Dean goes off-script and puts a gun to Chuck's head, bringing Chuck into the Winchesters' story. Chuck subsequently saves Sam just by being in the same motel room as the demon, because, as a prophet, he's protected by the Archangel Raphael. He's also susceptible to false visions, as is demonstrated when the angel Zachariah tricks him into sending the Winchesters to their father's storage locker to find the Michael Sword.

Despite their low sales, the Supernatural books have a passionately devoted following, so Chuck's number-one fan, Becky Rosen, throws a Supernatural convention, and after Chuck heroically battles a real ghost, he becomes romantically involved with her.

Their relationship doesn't last, and neither do his visions. After he finishes the story of how the Winchester brothers averted the Apocalypse, Chuck dons a white suit—and *disappears*. Was he actually God? Or maybe Chuck really died before his visions started, and with his heavenly task now completed, his time on Earth was up.

ROB BENEDICT

Of all the people on Earth, or at least in America, why was Chuck Shurley picked to write the Winchester Gospels? "That's definitely the question Chuck is always asking himself," says actor Rob Benedict. "He's like, 'Why me? I didn't ask for this.' I think that we always think of biblical figures like prophets and angels as these grandiose, larger-than-life things, but the way that Eric Kripke has imagined them, they're actually everyday people with normal desires and quirky traits and negative aspects and all that stuff that makes them human. It's interesting to make a prophet the most unlikely guy that you can imagine, someone who just has these visions; he's just a source. He didn't ask for it; it's just given to him. Deep down, Chuck's a tortured writer; he's wracked with self-doubt, and how it manifests itself is funny because here's this guy who's completely down on his luck, he's drunk, he's dirty, he's locked up in his house, and then he finds out that he's actually a Prophet of the Lord. It's really fun to play that guy and hang out [all day] in a bathrobe."

OPPOSITE, TOP: Three of Chuck Shurley's less-than-successful Supernatural *novel covers. LEFT: Chuck finds himself in the uncoveted role of being a Prophet of the Lord and author of the Winchester Gospels …*

BEHIND THE SCENES

ABOVE: Sam and Dean witness a soul's luminosity firsthand in season 5's "My Bloody Valentine." OPPOSITE: Hordes of demons escape from the Devil's Gate in the season 2 finale, "All Hell Breaks Loose, Part 2."

THE VFX DEPARTMENT

"A visual effect is anything that is augmented by a computer," explains visual-effects supervisor Ivan Hayden. The visual effects on *Supernatural* are amazing, especially considering the time and budget the TV show has to work with, but Hayden hopes you don't even notice his work. "Although we want people to like the effects and think about them afterward, we're an engine for the story, so our praise is no praise, because if anyone is stopping to say, 'Hey, the visual effects looks good,' if a visual effect takes anyone out of the story, then we've failed in our job. The hope is that everyone's concentrating on the story. In visual effects, we're sort of the unsung heroes, and that's fine with us."

Even though the seamless visual effects don't pull people out of the story, many of the things they're used for, such as Leviathan mouths and beheadings, are assumed to be done with computer graphics. However, there are many other subtle effects that viewers aren't likely to pick up on. For instance, one

of Hayden's favorite effects from season 2 was a dying plant in "Children Shouldn't Play with Dead Things." "We have a big 360-degree camera move on a potted plant that's sitting on the table," he explains, "and that potted plant didn't exist—we did the move without anything there, put the pot in, put the plant in, then withered it. People probably think, 'Oh, they did that with time lapse,' but it's all CG."

Likewise, for the scene in "No Exit" where the brothers climb down into the sewer, you practically expect them to get tangled in cobwebs, so when you see the creepy-crawlies you're likely surprised that they're cockroaches, but you never realize they're entirely CG critters. "For that scene we decided that cockroaches would be the best thing to do," reflects Hayden, "because if we were gonna go with spiders, you'd have only one and it's not as creepy."

And is there anything creepier than a haunted dollhouse? Okay, maybe there is—with a show like *Supernatural*, though,

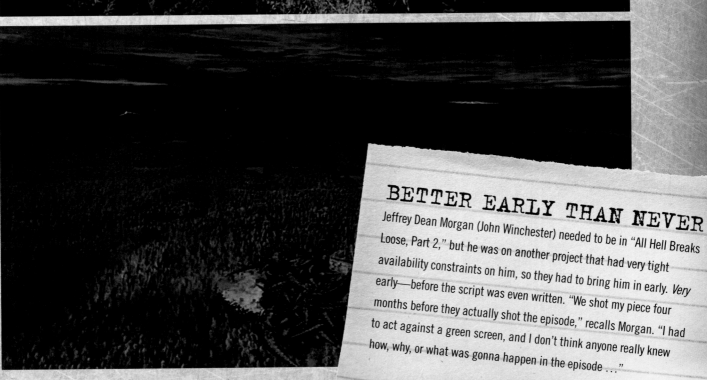

BETTER EARLY THAN NEVER

Jeffrey Dean Morgan (John Winchester) needed to be in "All Hell Breaks Loose, Part 2," but he was on another project that had very tight availability constraints on him, so they had to bring him in early. *Very early*—before the script was even written. "We shot my piece four months before they actually shot the episode," recalls Morgan. "I had to act against a green screen, and I don't think anyone really knew how, why, or what was gonna happen in the episode . . ."

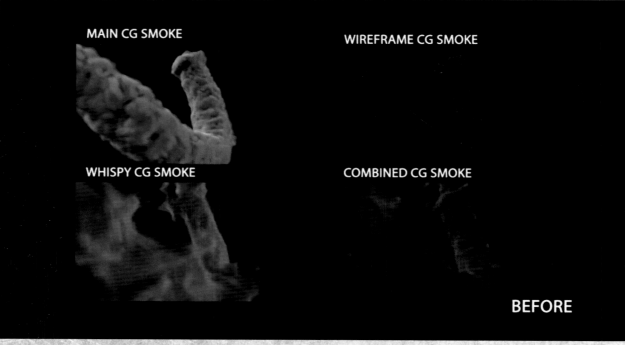

MAIN CG SMOKE

WIREFRAME CG SMOKE

WHISPY CG SMOKE

COMBINED CG SMOKE

BEFORE

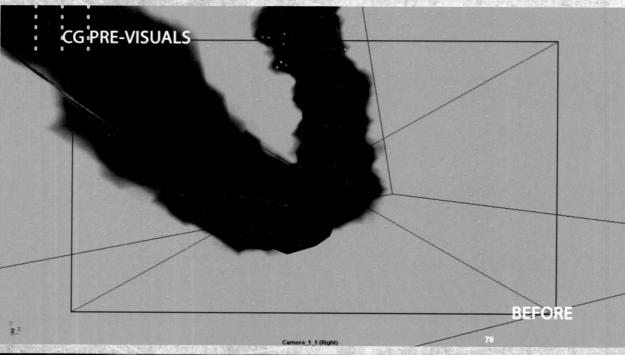

CG PRE-VISUALS

BEFORE

Camera_1_1 (Right)

78

AFTER

OPPOSITE: The complicated VFX process to make demon smoke travel look effortless and quick on-screen. ABOVE: The opulent dollhouse from the season 2 episode "Playthings."

Gore-Tastic Visual Effects

Creator Eric Kripke has fond memories of the decapitated female vampires in "Fresh Blood." "That was pretty wild," he reminisces. "The girls were wearing green hoods, and Ivan Hayden erased their heads and added the gore and the meat around their necks, so you could see their spinal column. I just loved that scene where Sam and Dean are having this emotional conversation and in the background you see this decapitated woman with her gored neck ..."

that's a tough question—but it's hard to watch "Playthings" and not get creeped out by the tiny swing set moving on its own. "'Playthings' was awesome for my department," says Hayden. "That dollhouse swing set wasn't supposed to be a visual-effects shot. The special-effects guys had it rigged up with some wires and it worked really well, but the way the swings were moving just didn't look like there was weight to them. We took the motion from the practical live-action swings and mimicked it in the little ones, and it looked really great."

The crew are constantly thinking of realistic little details like this, and they don't skimp on something just because there's no way of knowing the details for sure, such as what really happens when you kill a demon. In those instances, they come up with something plausible that looks good, too. For example, for the demon-killing-knife effect, Hayden says, "you can see the burning happening inside the body. We look at it as if the demon knife is killing a person on the molecular level."

Speaking of molecules, how many water molecules are there in a typical storm cloud? It's hard to say, but there are definitely hundreds of demons in the black cloud in "The Magnificent Seven." "We did that shot with three different clouds before Eric Kripke signed off on it," Hayden shares. "We were getting to the point where we were starting to get terrified, going, 'Oh no, what if he doesn't like this one?' But he went for it, and it set the tone for how the rest of the clouds have gone, including the 'Jus in Bello' gas station shot."

Even with the occasionally terrifying trial and error of creating new supernatural effects within a limited time frame, Hayden says, "this show is a dream come true for visual-effects guys because every episode, you have to create a monster, display its powers, and kill it. It never gets boring. We love them all."

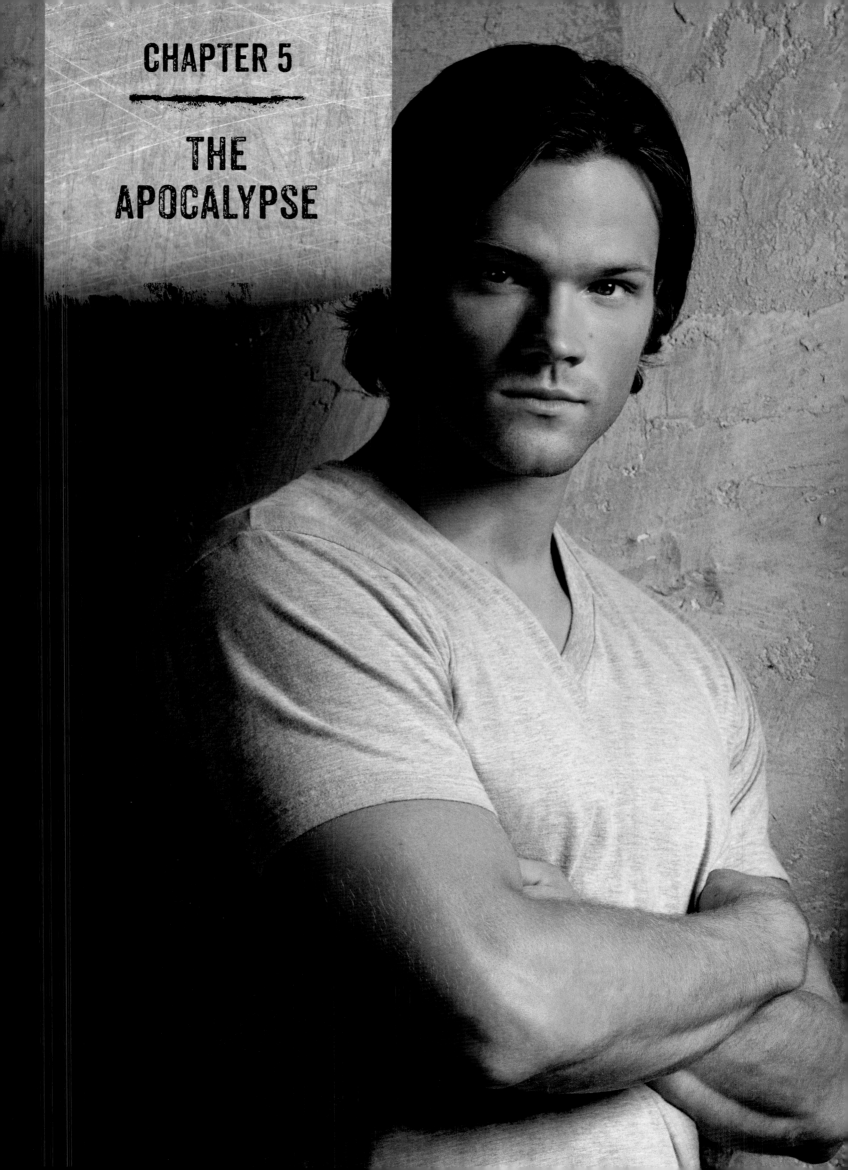

CHAPTER 5

THE APOCALYPSE

SEASON 5: THE STORY

Lucifer has risen. Trapped in the church where Sam killed Lilith and broke the final seal on Lucifer's cage, Sam and Dean Winchester expect to be Lucifer's first victims, but an unseen force suddenly teleports them to an airplane flying by the area.

They assume Castiel saved them, until they visit Chuck and learn that the Archangel Raphael smote Castiel as punishment for helping Dean try to stop Sam from freeing Lucifer. Zachariah arrives and demands that Dean help the angels fight Lucifer, but angry over the murder of Castiel, Dean banishes Zachariah. Nonetheless, when Chuck later sends the Winchesters a coded message through the *Supernatural* novels' number-one fan, Becky Rosen, Dean is anxious to find the Michael Sword to use against Lucifer. He holes up with Sam and Bobby in their latest hideout and eventually figures out that the sword is in his father's storage locker—and is suddenly attacked by Bobby Singer!

Turns out the demon Meg is after the Michael Sword, too, and ordered one of her minions to possess Bobby. Meg arrives as Bobby fights his demonic possession, turning the demon-killing knife on himself and saving Dean, but paralyzing himself from the waist down in the process. Desperate to get their hands on the sword, the brothers race to their father's lockup. But the cruel joke's on them: Dean *is* the Michael Sword. He's the Archangel Michael's chosen vessel for fighting Lucifer. He doesn't want to become an "angel condom," as he puts it, but Zachariah has a convincing sales pitch: he must say yes or watch his brother die a painful death while Dean himself suffers through advanced stomach cancer.

Castiel suddenly returns, saving Sam and Dean and banishing Zachariah. All signs point to an intervention by God Himself. Castiel has enough angel mojo left to carve Enochian sigils into Sam and Dean's ribs to hide them from Zachariah,

OPPOSITE: Dean and Sam arrive in a town controlled by paranoia and suspicion thanks to the Horseman War. TOP LEFT: Becky Rosen is Supernatural's—and Sam Winchester's—number-one fan. TOP RIGHT: Rufus Turner is cornered after the townspeople turn against each other as part of the Horseman War's plot to wreak havoc on Earth. CENTER LEFT: When Sam and Dean encounter Ellen Harvelle, she is not sure if her friends are themselves or demon-possessed. CENTER RIGHT: Sam and Dean prepare for the worst when they see the devastation wrought by the Horsemen War. ABOVE LEFT: Dean wakes up in a post-apocalyptic future where the United States is devastated with the Croatoan virus. ABOVE RIGHT: Future Castiel is no longer an angel and is instead a pacifist who is fond of orgies.

but now a rogue angel, he is mostly cut off from Heaven and doesn't have the power to repair Bobby's legs.

Sam admits to Dean that he is still addicted to demon blood and the feeling of power it gave him. He's tempted to bring his demonic powers back to full power to fight Lucifer, which scares both him and his brother. Dean still doesn't fully trust Sam because of what happened with Ruby. To avoid temptation, Sam quits hunting and Dean continues on alone. Unfortunately, Zachariah sends Dean to a future where Sam has said yes to Lucifer, thereby bringing on the Apocalypse. While possessed by Lucifer, Future Sam kills Future Dean. But instead of this incident leading Dean to agree to become Michael's vessel as Zachariah intended, it only convinces Dean that he needs to stick with Sam and keep his younger brother from going over to the dark side.

It seems every which way the Winchesters turn someone is trying to make one or both of them say yes to the archangels who want to inhabit their bodies. Lucifer brings the Four Horsemen of the Apocalypse onto the playing field, and Death turns Bobby's wife into a zombie with the hopes that she'll eat Bobby's brains and stop him from influencing Sam and Dean's decisions. When that doesn't work, Famine forces Sam to drink demon blood, thereby reawakening his demonic powers, but Sam disables Famine and willingly—and painfully—detoxes in Bobby's panic room. Still, the hits keep coming: even

their frenemy the Trickster wants them to play along and accept their destinies as vessels for Lucifer and Michael. He puts them in a TV land where Dean's favorite show, *Dr. Sexy, MD*, is real, Japanese game shows are painful, and Sam is a talking version of the Winchester car. After this unique torture, the Trickster reveals that he is an archangel, too: Gabriel. He ran away from his squabbling brothers, as he could not bear their constant fighting, but now he wants them to have a big showdown and get it over with.

Sam and Dean are angry and feel unsure which direction to turn. None of the supernatural creatures—angels, horsemen, and demons alike—seem to care that Michael and Lucifer's prize fight will kill billions of humans and destroy the world. How, exactly, can they stop Lucifer? Well, the Antichrist might be powerful enough, so when Sam and Dean hear about the discovery of the offspring of a demon-possessed human woman, they investigate. What they discover, however, is a scared, confused child—he turned Castiel into an action figure with a mere thought, after all—despite the fact that he has potential powers that could rival Lucifer's; better to just hide that game piece.

The brothers wonder if the Colt is the solution to their problem, but they have one big problem. Lilith's right-hand man, the Crossroads Demon Crowley, has possession of the gun. When they confront Crowley in his mansion, he shocks

OPPOSITE: Future Dean is a hardened, emotionally damaged version of his old self. TOP LEFT: Future Castiel is amused at the more optimistic incarnation of Dean from the past. TOP RIGHT: Lucifer has his first vessel on Earth, a once-devout man named Nick whose wife and young child were savagely murdered. ABOVE LEFT: Sam and Dean encounter the Antichrist, the child of a demon-possessed human woman. ABOVE RIGHT: The young Antichrist has enormous powers, as well as the choice to use them for good instead of evil. LEFT: Dean enters a magically enhanced poker game in order to win the use of Bobby's legs back.

ABOVE LEFT: Bobby's wife is back from the dead as a zombie who loves to bake pies for her husband and the Winchesters. TOP RIGHT: Bobby's time with his newly resurrected wife is limited, as she soon begins to exhibit the desire to eat human flesh. ABOVE, CENTER LEFT: Bobby makes a deal with Crowley for the use of his legs back. The price? A contract on his soul. ABOVE, CENTER RIGHT: Crowley has the Colt the Winchesters need to kill Lucifer with … ABOVE RIGHT: Too bad it has no effect on Lucifer or his vessel.

the Winchesters by happily giving them the Colt. Crowley believes Lucifer will wipe out all the demons along with the humans, and what good is that? Meg and her invisible Hellhounds nearly stop Sam and Dean from getting their shot at using the Colt on Lucifer, but Ellen and Jo Harvelle sacrifice themselves to clear a path for the brothers to Lucifer. Once they find him, Sam distracts Lucifer and Dean shoots the fallen angel in the head.

It *almost* works. The Colt bullet hurts Lucifer, but it doesn't kill him. It turns out that Lucifer is one of only five things in creation that the Colt can't kill.

To make matters worse, other monsters keep distracting the Winchesters from their research into ways to truly kill the Devil. They face off with vampires, pagan gods, ghosts, witches, a wraith that temporarily turns them insane, and the Whore of Babylon, too. Angel Anna has a clever way to stop Lucifer, but the brothers don't like her idea, as it involves traveling to the past and killing Mary and John Winchester so that they'll never give birth to Sam, Lucifer's chosen vessel. Sam and Dean fail to stop Anna, and in fact unwittingly give her what she wants: a

chance to kill Sam, which she does. But Michael possesses John and smites Anna, then gives Dean another opportunity to accept becoming Michael's true vessel before he brings Sam back to life. God could kill Lucifer, obviously, but when Sam and Dean are shot to death by fellow hunters and end up in Heaven, God sends them a message through Heaven's gardener, Joshua. He confirms that He put them on the plane that saved them from Lucifer, and He also resurrected Castiel, but that's as much help as He's willing to give, because God feels that stopping the Apocalypse is not His problem.

Zachariah resurrects Sam and Dean's half-brother Adam as a new possibility for Michael's vessel. The Winchesters rush to Adam's rescue, only to discover it was a trap; Adam was just bait to lure Dean into Zachariah's newest plan. Shockingly, Dean agrees to become the Michael Sword. He's convinced that Michael is the only one who can kill Lucifer, and he wants to kill the Devil before he somehow tricks Sam into becoming his vessel. Only, Dean can't really do it. Sam trusted him not to say yes, and he can't let his brother down like that. Screw destiny.

Dean has a new idea: if Michael, being an archangel, can kill Lucifer, maybe Gabriel can as well. Unfortunately, Gabriel dies trying, but not before he passes on a message to the Winchesters: if they steal the Four Horsemen's rings, they can use the magic of the combined objects to send Lucifer back to Hell. They'd rather kill Satan, but Michael has now taken Adam as his vessel; the Winchesters are out of time and out of options. With Crowley's help once more—which includes borrowing Bobby's soul in exchange for healing his legs and locating Death—Sam and Dean obtain the rings, but there's still the small problem of getting Lucifer back into his cage, as there is no way he will go willingly. Which leaves only one option: Sam has to become his vessel and throw himself into Hell.

Sam feels tremendous guilt for freeing Lucifer and believes he has to set things straight. Dean hates this plan, but even he can't think of any other way to save the world. As soon as Sam says yes to Lucifer, Dean opens the portal to Hell, but Lucifer suppresses Sam's consciousness and takes the rings from Dean. It seems all is lost.

But Dean doesn't give up. Lucifer is ready to fight Michael, but Castiel uses a Holy Fire Molotov cocktail to temporarily send Michael away. Lucifer snaps his fingers and Castiel explodes. The Devil is done being nice. He snaps Bobby's neck and beats Dean within an inch of his life. Seeing all this enrages Sam, and he wrestles control of his conscience back from the Devil. He opens the portal again and lunges toward it. Michael returns and tries to stop him, but it's too late. Pulling Michael/Adam with him, Sam plunges into Hell.

God resurrects Castiel once more, who in turn resurrects Bobby, then heals Dean. But Castiel can't heal the hole in Dean's heart. Sam is gone, burning in Hell for all eternity.

Elsewhere, Chuck finishes typing up Sam and Dean's story, then vanishes. He's obviously more than a prophet, but is he God? Will he bring Sam back from Hell? It turns out that *someone* does. Dean doesn't know it, but as he settles into a new life with his old flame Lisa and her son Ben, hoping that an apple pie life will help heal that hole in his heart, his brother is standing outside the window watching him in enigmatic silence . . .

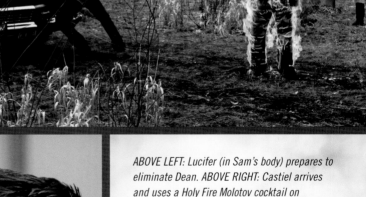

ABOVE LEFT: Lucifer (in Sam's body) prepares to eliminate Dean. ABOVE RIGHT: Castiel arrives and uses a Holy Fire Molotov cocktail on Michael's vessel. LEFT: Zachariah is tired of bargaining with Dean and prepares to smite him—but Dean beats him to it and kills the angel with Castiel's blade.

TOP LEFT: Lucifer confronts Dean in the young Winchester's dream to tell him that becoming his vessel is inevitable. ABOVE LEFT: Actor Mark Pellegrino relaxes between takes on the set of "Hammer of the Gods" in this continuity photo from the costume department. ABOVE RIGHT: Lucifer and Sam finally meet—and Sam finally says "yes" to becoming his vessel.

LUCIFER: KING OF HELL

Lucifer. Satan. The Devil. Beelzebub. Serpent King. Lord of the Flies. Prince of Darkness. Father of Lies. Ruler of Hell. Call him what you will, just don't call him a demon. For the most famous demon of all is in fact *not* a demon. He is a fallen angel. A fallen *archangel*. He did, however, create demons, and for that God imprisoned him in Hell.

Lucifer truly believes that he was wronged by God for not bowing down to humans, who he sees as flawed, violent, fragile little creatures. When Sam Winchester frees him from his cage, Lucifer wants revenge on humans, on his archangel brothers, and on God himself. As an archangel supercharged with over a millennia of pent-up anger, he's too powerful to

be properly contained by his first meat-suit, a once-devout man named Nick, although he still manages to survive a point-blank shot to the head from the Colt. After he convinces Sam to become his new vessel, Lucifer reveals his greatest weakness: vanity. He overestimates his suppression of Sam's will and underestimates the power of familial love, losing control of Sam's body long enough for Sam to drag Lucifer back to Hell.

Lucifer tortures Sam so much in Hell that even after his soul is restored to his body by Death, Sam continues to hallucinate Lucifer's devilish presence—that is, until Castiel takes these visions away as an act of contrition.

MARK PELLEGRINO

Like most actors, Mark Pellegrino (Lucifer's vessel, Nick) enjoys playing villains, but he says he never even imagined he'd get the chance to play the biggest and baddest big bad of them all, the Devil. As much fun as it might have been to play the ultimate villain as evil incarnate, Pellegrino found the writers' interpretation of the Prince of Darkness as a misunderstood angel much more interesting. "He is kind of the prince of the world," Pellegrino believes. A prince that feels wronged by the king (God). "I just looked at it from worldly standards as a debt that needs to be paid. That's what I was going for." Of course, the Devil's also known as the Prince of Lies, but Pellegrino says Lucifer doesn't *need* to lie. Instead, he's "utterly and totally honest."

In the spirit of total honesty, Pellegrino admits that it was "a bit uncomfortable" walking around in clothes soaked with the pagan gods' blood and guts in "Hammer of the Gods" "because that stuff is corn syrup and something else, so it's really sticky, and then it gets stiff as a board." Not that Pellegrino didn't enjoy smashing through the assembled ranks of pagan gods. He'd expected, however, that he'd get to put the smackdown on the top pagan god. "I wonder why Zeus wasn't there?" he muses. "I wonder, why Mercury instead? Why did the messenger of the gods get in there, but not Zeus?"

It's interesting to ponder whether Lucifer could have taken out Zeus while in the Nick meat-suit, which was rapidly deteriorating at that point in time. Then again, he did take on his powerful archangel brother Gabriel. Despite the fact that Lucifer's transfer from Nick to Sam Winchester meant the death of Pellegrino's stint as the Devil (at least in the nonhallucinatory sense), Pellegrino says, "I like the way the main archangels were trying to inhabit the Winchester brothers. I find it very interesting that the brothers were engaged in this at the head of the battle." What Pellegrino was most interested in knowing after season 5 wrapped was if he'd get to come back to the show. It's always possible Lucifer could escape Hell again. And if he did, he could resurrect Nick's body as a means to bring Pellegrino back, too, but the actor doesn't think it's likely. "Where do you go after the Apocalypse?" he asks. Well, you go to Purgatory, obviously! But even though Pellegrino returned as the hallucinatory incarnation of Sam's tortured soul, the real Lucifer is still trapped in Hell, hoping one day for a repeat performance.

TOP: Dean summons Death and the reaper Tessa to make a deal to restore Sam's missing soul. ABOVE LEFT: Death points out the fine print for making a deal with him. ABOVE RIGHT: Dean gets up close and personal with Death—the elder Winchester is perhaps the only human being who can.

The Rings of Destiny

Each of the Four Horsemen wears a mystical ring, which, while not the source of their supernatural abilities, appears to help them focus their powers, although Death needs his ring much less than his brothers do. War wears a simple gold ring (adornments would no doubt get in the way in the midst of battle), Famine wears a silver ring with intricate engravings and a black stone, Pestilence wears a silver ring with elaborate engravings and a green stone, and Death wears a silver ring with symbolic engravings and a white stone.

The four rings have a special bond—when joined together they become a key powerful enough to open a portal to Lucifer's cage in Hell.

THE FOUR HORSEMEN

The Four Horsemen—War, Famine, Pestilence, and Death—are destructive forces of nature. When they show themselves to humans, they do so with great dramatic flare: War has been seen riding a red horse and driving a red Ford Mustang; Famine a black horse and a black Cadillac Escalade; Pestilence a pale green horse and a sickly green AMC Hornet; and Death a white horse and a white Cadillac Eldorado. All of the Horsemen can teleport, and they each have special supernatural talents: War reads minds and gives people hallucinations that make them fight with one another; Famine consumes souls (human or demon) and makes people so hungry for the things they crave the most that they're willing to kill for them; Pestilence creates horrific and incurable diseases; and Death commands reapers and raises the dead.

Throughout the history of humankind, the Four Horsemen have always been around, but Lucifer gathers them to him in preparation for the Apocalypse. War, Famine, and Pestilence don't seem to mind following Lucifer's orders, but Death—who is far more powerful than the other Horsemen—does not like being bound to Lucifer. And while the other Horsemen are greatly weakened from losing their magic rings to the Winchester brothers, Death willingly gives Dean his ring, as the combined rings are the key to sending Lucifer back to his cage in Hell.

The Four Horsemen go their own ways after the failed Apocalypse attempt, although if the Winchester brothers ever see them again, they'd be wise to avoid them. Death, on the other hand, is practically on Dean's speed dial list. The elder Winchester calls on the powerful Horseman to retrieve both Sam and Adam's souls from Hell, to build a wall in his wayward brother's mind to protect him from the damaged parts of his soul, and to stop an out-of-control Castiel after he absorbs all the souls from Purgatory. Death doesn't save Adam or reap Castiel, but he does build a wall in Sam's mind after restoring his damaged soul. Despite the friction every time Dean summons death, he's batting .500 and should consider himself lucky to have encountered Death three times and lived to tell the tale . . .

TOP LEFT: Sign for the Aardvark Motel, from episode 207, "The Usual Suspects." TOP RIGHT: Sign for Larsen's Landing, from episode 214, "Born Under a Bad Sign."
ABOVE LEFT: Sign for the Pack 'Em Inn Motel, from episode 603, "Weekend at Bobby's." ABOVE RIGHT: Sign for the Rainbow Motel, from episode 404, "Metamorphosis."

(TEMPORARY) HOME SWEET HOMES: THE MOTELS OF *SUPERNATURAL*

One of the most iconic things about *Supernatural* are the motel rooms that grace nearly every episode. "They have become our trademark," agrees production designer Jerry Wanek. With 149 episodes and around that many motel rooms, Wanek says it's become a fun challenge to keep them fresh and make them different. But they don't make them different simply for the sake of being different. "The thing that drives me crazy, as far as watching other shows, is seeing people that are just trying to be different," Wanek says, "because if it's out of context or if the colors don't work together or if the scale isn't right, then it just sticks out like a sore thumb. On the other hand, you can get really outrageous

as long as you incorporate it into the rest of the theme, as long as the scale is right, as long as it's complemented by other outrageous things so that it all blends into one. That's one of the things that we stress here, and our motel rooms are a great example of that. We create really outrageous motel rooms, but everything in them works together. A lot of thought goes into our screens, our color combinations, our lamps and bedding. No matter how wild we get with the colors or shapes, they work together as an ensemble, so it's believable as a really funky motel. But if you just take one element and put it in a normal motel room, people go, 'What is that doing there?' It's really important that you really go for it. You've got to carry

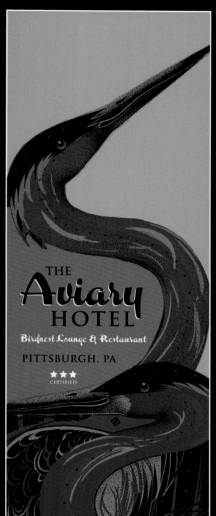

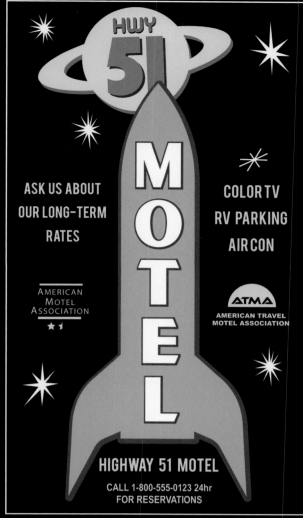

ABOVE LEFT: Sign for the Aviary Hotel, from episode 310, "Dream a Little Dream of Me." ABOVE CENTER: A cool atomic-age image of a rocket sets the stage for the Highway 51 Motel. ABOVE RIGHT: Sign for the Tall Totem Lodge, from episode 408, "Wishful Thinking."

the design all the way through to the telephone to the towel bar, to whatever. It's all got to work together."

And while it has to work together in a way that looks good to the audience, the rooms also have to be functional sets that aren't so outrageous that they distract the actors from what they're doing. "If I don't give the actors the right place to perform, to do their craft, and to make them believe they're totally in that character, then I haven't done my job," Wanek points out. Along with thinking of the actors, Wanek keeps the directors' needs in mind, too. One of the things he's found they use a lot is the motel room screens, which have become iconic in their own right. "The screens are a wonderful element

for directors to be able to pan through," he feels. They're also references to the inspirations for the motel rooms. "For example, in the Brew City motel, we did this whole screen with these lit beer bottles and beer taps that were also backlit, and it became quite a nice little piece."

"I like working on the screens because you know that they will get seen," comments graphic designer Mary-Ann Liu. "They really add to the feel of the set." As do the ubiquitous tent cards, which Liu and her fellow graphic designer, Lee-Anne Elaschuk, create. "We do a lot of Americana," Liu points out, "but we've also done a number of high-end places. We have that range; it's kind of extreme, and I like that. There was

TOP LEFT: From episode 711, "Adventures in Babysitting." TOP RIGHT: From episode 109, "Home." ABOVE LEFT: From episode 303, "Bad Day at Black Rock."
CENTER RIGHT: From episode 602, "Two and a Half Men." ABOVE RIGHT: From episode 110, "Asylum." OPPOSITE, TOP: From episode 722, "There Will Be Blood."
OPPOSITE, BOTTOM: From episode 719, "Of Grave Importance."

a Mike's Travel Inn [in "Point of No Return"] that I did where, for me, the colors are just hideous, but it fits the scene because it describes what it is: a very low-budget, utilitarian kind of thing. You grunge it up and use colors that are jarring to bring about that mood. The opposite is the really fancy Elysium Hotel [in "Hammer of the Gods"]. What a beautiful set. That hotel is just incredible."

Another high-end example comes from "When the Levee Breaks." "It was so different," Wanek says. "It has the screens, it has funky wallpaper, but it has some very elegant finishes like the leather-upholstered wall above the headboard. It's very

similar to the funky stuff that we do in that it has many different elements, and it's got the same amount of eye-catching stuff, but it's all taken to the next level, so that was fun."

Whether the motel rooms are high-end, grungy, or funky cool, the fans look forward to seeing what Wanek and his crew will do next. "It's a fun challenge," Wanek concludes. "It's funny as the rest of the crew also gets really excited about the premiere of the new motels, because they never know what to expect . . ."

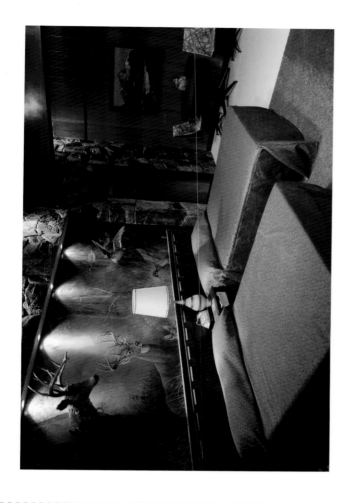

Rainbow Motel
Carthage, Missouri
404: "Metamorphosis"

SUPERNATURAL: TM & © Warner Bros. Entertainment Inc.
(s12)

6 Pines Motel
Portland, OR
612: "Like a Virgin"

SUPERNATURAL: TM & © Warner Bros. Entertainment Inc.
(s12)

The Big Ride Motel
Providence, Rhode Island
213: "Houses of the Holy"

SUPERNATURAL: TM & © Warner Bros. Entertainment Inc.
(s12)

Route 66 Motel
Lansing, Michigan
602: "Two and a Half Men"

BEHIND THE SCENES

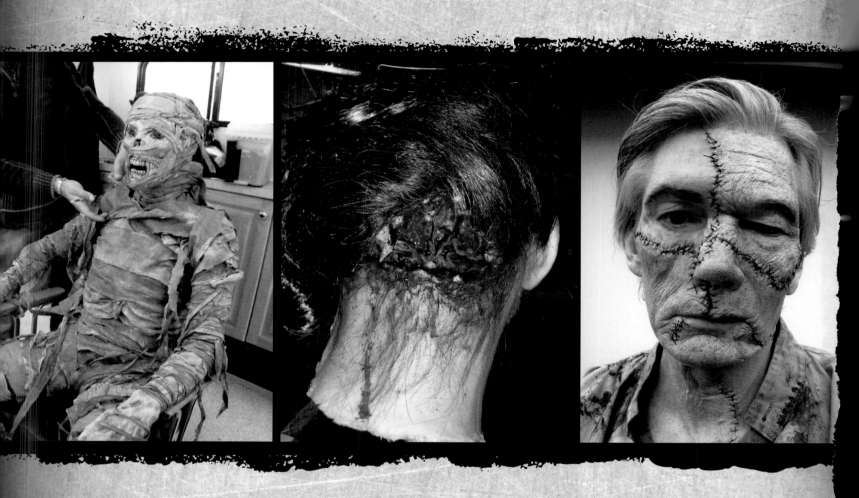

ABOVE LEFT: The Mummy (Geoff Redknap) from episode 405, "Monster Movie," is ready for his close-up! ABOVE CENTER: The pituitary glands are missing from this unfortunate brain in a model built for episode 703, "The Girl Next Door." ABOVE RIGHT: Actor Billy Drago poses in his Doc Benton makeup for episode 315, "Time Is on My Side." OPPOSITE, CENTER LEFT: Decomposed party guests from season 3's "Ghostfacers." OPPOSITE, BOTTOM LEFT: The mottled wretch's exposed insides await the Winchesters' examination. OPPOSITE, BOTTOM RIGHT: The distinctive Amazonian symbol carved in a poor victim's flesh from episode 713, "The Slice Girls."

PROSTHETICS AND MAKEUP EFFECTS

"Working on *Supernatural* is always exhilarating," says Toby Lindala, head of special-effects makeup. "As soon as we get a concept, we hit the ground running and do the best we can in about a week and a half to two weeks. I feed on that adrenaline, on that excitement." Not surprisingly, Toby Lindala got into the monster-making business because he's a fan of monster movies. "The early Universal films really affected me when I was younger," he says, "so working on 'Monster Movie' was awesome. That was a big one for us."

After six seasons with *Supernatural*, Lindala Schminken FX continues to find ways to keep the monster designs fresh. "We have a lot of in-house meetings and bat around ideas," Lindala says. "I've got a lot of great artists on staff. We're excited about keeping our passion alive, so we'll play with

new materials, like the 3D transfer appliances, which were designed and created specifically for Misha Collins (Castiel), who degrades throughout the season 7 opener. They all glue together in a pattern.

"We push things on *Supernatural*. We go for the shocks." Like in the kitchen scene from "Hammer of the Gods," where there's a severed human hand on a chopping board. "We had the ragged end of the hand with bone and flesh and chopping marks," Lindala recalls. "We had a pump for blood as well, so we had this growing pool of blood, as though it had just happened.

"We're really in sync with [the *Supernatural* producers], and as the seasons have progressed we've had more and more satisfaction all around. I'm really thankful for that."

The Mottled Wretch

Ever eaten a Turducken Slammer? You probably won't want to after watching "How to Make Friends and Influence Monsters." In that episode, the triple meat sandwich is laced with a Leviathan-concocted additive that inadvertently turns people into monsters that'll eat pretty much anything, from pinecones to cat heads, although they're messy eaters, wasting perfectly good human ears by dropping them on the ground. The script describes the monster that Bobby shot out of a tree as a "mottled wretch," and the makeup-effects crew ran with that description. They created a full facial prosthetic for the actor portraying the wretch to wear. The customized mask included eye pieces, but fortunately that wasn't a problem. "She sees virtually nothing," Lindala says. "Luckily, she was a stunt actress, because she's blind while she's taking those gunshots."

CHAPTER 6

FINDING PURGATORY

SEASON 6: THE STORY

A year after dragging Lucifer back into Hell, Sam mysteriously reappears, saving Dean from a djinn attack that shatters his brother's newfound domestic bliss with Lisa and Ben. Dean should be overcome with joy, but instead he's suspicious of exactly how his brother escaped. Sam claims not to know, as does Castiel, who further rules out God as Sam's savior. It doesn't help matters that Sam returned from Hell almost immediately after his battle with Lucifer, allowing his brother to mourn him unnecessarily for a whole year and claiming that he did so for altruistic reasons; he wanted Dean to be free of the hunting life and able to enjoy a normal existence with his new family. Dean's suspicions kick into overdrive when he discovers that his grandfather Samuel has also been mysteriously resurrected. What's more, the younger Sam has been hunting alongside him and several cousins from the Campbell side of the family.

Now that Dean's in the loop, Sam's not shy about pulling him back into the hunting life the moment a baby shapeshifter gets a little colicky, which leads to an encounter with the Alpha Shapeshifter, the very first and strongest of its kind. Despite Dean's reluctance to leave Lisa and Ben, he knows that hunting alongside Sam is where he belongs. He takes the tarp off the Winchester car and hits the road.

Meanwhile, Bobby teams up with Rufus to fight an okami, then discovers a way to blackmail Crowley into reversing the deal on his soul. Since demons are essentially just ghosts twisted into evil spirits, salting and burning their bones will banish them from the Earth. Sam and Dean fly to Scotland and dig up Crowley's bones, which they hand over to the Crossroads Demon in exchange for destroying the contract on Bobby's soul.

The brothers fight a lamia (a humanoid monster that feeds on the hearts of its victims) and help Castiel discover that the rogue angel Balthazar stole an arsenal of heavenly weapons, but something seems wrong with Sam. There is something off about him that Dean can't quite put his finger on. Dean's fears are realized when Sam purposely stands by and *lets* him get turned into a bloodsucker while hunting the Alpha Vampire. Thinking he has no choice but to let Sam chop his head off, Dean runs away to say good-bye to Lisa first, but this touching reunion turns out to be a very bad idea. Overcome by vampiric bloodlust, he nearly bites Lisa and irreparably damages their relationship by

OPPOSITE: Dean can't figure out what's different about Sam lately, and he's not sure he even wants to know … TOP LEFT: A shocked Dean is reintroduced to his very much alive grandfather Samuel Campbell, whose death he witnessed when Castiel sent him to the past. TOP RIGHT: Grandpa Campbell is hiding a dark secret from his grandsons. ABOVE LEFT: Bobby summons Crowley to demand that the demon destroy the contract on his soul. ABOVE: An Alpha Shapeshifter in the guise of Dean Winchester … LEFT: Crowley is far from pleased to be summoned by Bobby …

TOP: Sam, Dean, and Castiel arrive at Balthazar's protected mansion. ABOVE LEFT: Fueled by his suspicions, Dean demands Sam tell him the truth about his emotionless behavior. ABOVE RIGHT: Sam and Dean arrive in a sleepy town to investigate a series of UFO sightings.

roughly pushing young Ben away. To his great surprise and relief, when he returns to his motel room, Dean finds his grandfather waiting with a cure for vampirism. Sam denies purposely letting Dean get turned, arguing that he was frozen in shock, but Dean's mistrust festers and comes to a boil when the Goddess of Truth, Veritas, freaks out over the fact that she can't make Sam tell the unvarnished truth. Dean knocks Sam out, ties him up, and gets Castiel to examine him. Castiel shoves his hand inside Sam's chest and learns the horrifying truth: Sam has no soul!

Sam convinces them that he is more machine than monster, and while he no longer has any feelings like love or compassion, he still has an unquenchable desire to hunt the evil creatures that roam the earth. With that mystery solved, another is soon revealed: Samuel was resurrected by Crowley, but to what purpose? It is revealed that the Crossroads Demon wants to tap Grandpa Campbell's hunting skills, and by extension Sam and Dean's as well, in order to capture as many alpha monsters as possible. The alphas know how to find Purgatory, which is essentially the afterlife for monsters, and

Crowley wants its sinister denizens for himself. Following Lucifer's incarceration, Crowley crowned himself King of Hell, and he's ready to expand his kingdom into Purgatory.

Sam and Dean's journey takes an odd detour through the realm of faeries when Dean is apparently abducted by aliens. Things only get weirder when he's attacked by a tiny, naked flying lady who glows and a vicious Redcap faerie, while Sam encounters elves and a leprechaun. They soon learn that the faeries have been using misinformation for decades and disguising stories of their existence as UFO sightings and alien abductions. Despite this unsettling discovery, what bothers Dean the most is that soulless Sam was having sex rather than trying to rescue him from his alien abductors. Unfortunately, there's no time for the brothers to have a heart-to-heart talk, as Dean teams up with the demon Meg to go after Crowley, believing the scheming demon can retrieve Sam's soul from Lucifer's cage in Hell. Unbeknownst to Dean and Meg, however, they are walking into a trap, and soon discover a shocking truth: Samuel sold them all out to Crowley and cares more about resurrecting his beloved daughter than about the lives of his grandsons. Sam, Dean, and Meg fight off ghouls, Hellhounds, and their demon-possessed cousin Christian Campbell before finally managing to capture Crowley with a Devil's Trap, only to discover that the Crossroads Demon doesn't have enough power to wrestle Sam's soul away from Lucifer. Castiel appears with Crowley's bones (which apparently weren't well hidden) and burns them up, seemingly destroying the King of Hell.

Dean can only think of one other creature powerful enough to retrieve Sam's soul: Death. Dean takes the drastic measure of getting an old doctor friend of the family to kill him so that he can speak to Death, begging the most notorious of the Four Horsemen to make Sam whole again. Sam, on the other hand, has come to accept his unnatural state and is afraid of getting his humanity back, so he asks Balthazar for a spell to keep his soul out of his body. The problem is he has to sacrifice his surrogate father, Bobby, to make the dark magic work. Of course, this isn't a problem for the unfeeling Sam, which is exactly why Dean is so desperate to get his sibling's soul back. Fortunately, Dean is just

in time to rescue Bobby, but Death wants something in return for restoring his brother's soul: Dean must wear Death's ring and experience what it's like to be a reaper. He does a less-than-stellar job, but Death is nonetheless impressed and returns Sam's soul. There is, of course, a catch: Sam's soul is so damaged from a year of being tortured by Lucifer that it will drive Sam crazy once it's restored, so Death puts up a wall in Sam's mind to prevent this from happening. However, there is no guarantee the wall will not crumble eventually.

Regardless of this potential threat to his sanity, Sam is finally himself again, and the brothers get back to doing what they do best: hunting. They hunt dragons—yes, *dragons*—a giant spider monster, and a ghost that possesses mannequins as well as the Winchester car, and they even take on Fate. The Winchester brothers have been to Heaven and Hell and back, Dean's been to faerie land, and they know Purgatory exists, and yet, despite this, the boys could never be prepared for what happens next.

Balthazar gives them a key to one of Heaven's safeguards that contains weapons and flings the Winchesters into an alternate

TOP LEFT: Castiel and Crowley discuss their shady deal over Eve's corpse in Crowley's secret laboratory. TOP RIGHT: A detail of one of Crowley's monster anatomy books. ABOVE LEFT: Castiel and company arrive at Crowley's secret compound to confront the Crossroads Demon … ABOVE RIGHT: But Hellhounds soon make their mission much more complicated.

TOP LEFT: Meg volunteers to destroy the Hellhounds so Dean, Sam, and Castiel can get to Crowley. TOP RIGHT: Bobby and Dean distract themselves with a potential case while waiting for Sam to wake up after Death restores his soul. ABOVE LEFT: Dean and Death go nose-to-nose as Dean asks the Horseman to return Sam's soul to his body. ABOVE RIGHT: Sam greets Dean and Bobby in an emotional reunion after Death restores the younger Winchester's soul.

reality where their lives are a TV show but they're not hunters—they're *actors*. Archangel Raphael sends Virgil, an angel assassin, after them, but Virgil's no match for Sam and Dean in this reality, which happens to have no magic. Nonetheless, Virgil escapes with the key and, after killing "Castiel" actor Misha Collins, he uses the actor's blood to somehow contact Raphael and arrange for another portal to be opened. He then commandeers human firearms and blasts his way through Eric Kripke, Bob Singer, Kevin Parks, and Lou Bollo. Sam and Dean ambush Virgil, retrieve the key, and jump through another portal to their own reality, leaving Virgil behind. Raphael is waiting for them, but makes a hasty retreat when Castiel arrives and reveals that he has control of the heavenly weapons.

With the tide of the war in Heaven turning in Castiel's favor, a new war is brewing on Earth. Crowley's been wiping out monsters and torturing alphas, and it's caught the notice of Eve, the Mother of All Monsters. *No one* messes with her children. She arrives from Purgatory in the vessel of a virgin female and begins creating new offspring with the ultimate intention of creating the perfect monster. She starts small, infecting a trucker with a slug-sized parasite that makes him kill his wife. The same little monster (which Dean dubs a

"Khan worm") goes on to infect Dean, who unfortunately kills his cousin Gwen Campbell. It next infects Samuel, who Sam kills without remorse before infecting Bobby, who tragically kills Rufus. Eve's next trick is to unleash a vampire-wraith hybrid, which Sam and Dean track down. They run into Eve instead, who asks the Winchesters to bring Crowley to her, claiming he isn't dead after all, but they refuse. Angry, Eve bites Dean, but he has a surprise in store—he's ingested phoenix ash, which is deathly poisonous to her. Before arriving to track down Eve's newest hybrid, Castiel had sent Sam and Dean into the past to obtain phoenix ash from Samuel Colt himself, and so Dean was highly prepared for his confrontation with Eve.

But even though Eve is now dead, Crowley is still alive, and still trying to break into Purgatory. What's worse: Castiel is helping him. They plan to steal all the monster souls from Purgatory—half for Crowley to cement his lock on Hell's throne, and half for Castiel to use to kick Raphael out of Heaven. Sam and Dean are devastated by Castiel's dark dealings, but the angel believes the ends—stopping Raphael from freeing Lucifer again—justifies the means. The alpha monsters are a dead end for this mission, as none will reveal the location of Purgatory—or

TOP LEFT: Sam is thrown for a loop when he is greeted lovingly by his "wife," actress Genevieve Padalecki. TOP RIGHT: Bobby comforts a mortally wounded Dr. Eleanor Visyak. ABOVE LEFT: A demon-possessed Lisa threatens to kill her meat-suit and her son Ben. ABOVE CENTER: Raphael (in a new vessel) arrives to aid Crowley in stopping a renegade Castiel. ABOVE RIGHT: Castiel is about to absorb millions of souls and declare himself the new king of Heaven ...

how to access it—to Crowley, but it transpires that author H. P. Lovecraft briefly opened a portal to Purgatory and a monster slipped through. Castiel abducts this creature, which took human form and happens to be a past lover of Bobby's named Eleanor Visyak, and he and Crowley torture her until she gives them the information they need.

After dealing with Eve, the Winchesters feel that opening another portal to Purgatory will only end badly, so they are willing to do whatever it takes to stop that from happening. Castiel won't let Crowley kill Sam and Dean, so the demon kidnaps Lisa and Ben as leverage to make Dean back off. Sam and Dean rescue Lisa and Ben, although not before Lisa is possessed by a demon and nearly takes her own life. Castiel heals Lisa, then erases her and Ben's memories of Dean at his request. Sam is appalled, but Dean feels it is the only way to keep them from being put in danger again.

Balthazar gives Sam and Dean Castiel's location, but Castiel finds out and, angry over the betrayal, kills his angelic brother. To stop Sam and Dean from interfering, Castiel removes the wall that Death put in Sam's mind sending him into a coma, where he battles his soulless self and the part of him that was

tortured in Hell. Seeing his brother trapped in mental anguish nearly immobilizes Dean, but Bobby convinces him to go after Castiel and stop the angel's plan.

Castiel tries double-crossing Crowley, but Crowley double-double-crosses him by bringing in Raphael. Castiel hands Crowley the jar of blood extracted from a Purgatory monster that is required to open the gateway, and vanishes. Dean and Bobby arrive, but are unable to stop Crowley from performing the ritual to access Purgatory. The only thing is, nothing happens. Castiel has given Crowley a jar full of dog blood. Triumphant, Castiel returns imbued with the power of millions of souls from Purgatory. Crowley flees, but Raphael is not so lucky, and with a snap of Castiel's fingers, he is obliterated. With this decisive victory, Dean tries to convince Castiel that the monster souls are no longer needed and that it would be dangerous to try to contain that much power, but Castiel disagrees and refuses to send the souls back to Purgatory. Sam—now conscious and appearing to be mentally stable—sneaks in and stabs Castiel with an angel-killing blade, but it doesn't work. Castiel is no longer an angel and believes he is now God. He commands Sam, Dean, and Bobby to bow down and profess their love to him, or they will be destroyed.

THE CAMPBELLS: HUNTERS OF OLD

Until the events of "In the Beginning," Sam and Dean Winchester believed that their mother's demonic death in Sam's nursery had simply been a case of being in the wrong place at the wrong time, and that their father's quest for vengeance is what led the Winchester family into the monster-hunting life. But that's not even close to the truth. Their mother, Mary, and their grandparents, Deanna and Samuel Campbell, were all hunters long before John Winchester became one.

In fact, the Campbells are a family line of hunters going back further than the first settlers of America, some of whom were hacking the heads off of vampires on the *Mayflower*. Despite their hunting pedigree, they are not immune to demonic dangers: Deanna gets killed by Azazel; Samuel gets possessed and killed by Azazel; Mary makes a deal with Azazel, trading John Winchester's life for access to baby Sam, only to be murdered by Azazel herself years later; Ed and Robert Campbell get killed by Azazel to keep John Winchester off the demon's trail; cousin Christian Campbell gets possessed by a demon and spies on his hunting kin; and Samuel is resurrected by Crowley and makes a deal with the Crossroads Demon, agreeing to capture alpha monsters in exchange for Crowley bringing his daughter Mary back to life.

When Dean encounters his resurrected grandfather, Samuel brags about his hunting know-how, boasting, "I'll show you tricks your daddy never even dreamed of . . ." And he does. When Dean gets turned into a vampire, for example, Samuel actually pulls a cure for vampirism out of his bag of tricks.

As talented a hunter as Samuel is, alpha monsters are formidable foes, so he surrounds himself with other Campbells, notably Christian, Gwen, Mark, and Johnny . . . and, of course, Sam and Dean. Even still, the Campbells find themselves almost outmatched by the monsters: a djinn kills Johnny; the Alpha Shapeshifter kills Mark; and the Alpha Vampire kills Christian, although the demon possessing him holds his meat-suit together until Dean uses the demon-killing knife on his cousin.

Ultimately, though, Samuel didn't have any tricks for fighting a brand-new monster he and his fellow hunters encountered. The Mother of All Monsters' parasitic Khan worm first gets into Dean, making him kill Gwen, then it gets into Samuel, leaving Sam no choice but to kill his own grandfather. With all the Campbells wiped out, only Sam and Dean remain to honor their family's hunting legacy.

OPPOSITE: The new generation of Campbell hunters: Christian, Dean Winchester, Gwen, Samuel, Sam Winchester, and Mark. TOP LEFT: Samuel is a study in mistrust and overprotectiveness, but his hunting skills are unmatched. TOP CENTER: Deanna is a compassionate, sensitive, and strong hunter in her own right. TOP RIGHT: Mary Campbell is destined for greatness as a hunter herself—except she doesn't want any part of her family's unusual legacy. ABOVE: A candid shot of Jared, Jensen, and Mitch Pileggi (Samuel Campbell).

HEAVENLY WEAPONS

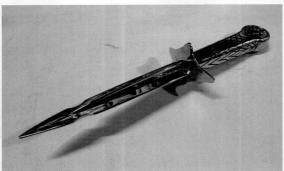

TOP LEFT: The sleek, silver, dangerous beauty of an angel-killing blade. ABOVE: The heavenly blade for episode 617, "My Heart Will Go On." ABOVE RIGHT: Meg wields an angel-killing blade; only, she is using it against other demons in her mission to protect Castiel.

BLADE DESIGN

"For episode 617, 'My Heart Will Go On,' we created the new heavenly blade," notes property master Christopher Cooper. "This was a collaboration in terms of design—the art department came up with the original design and then the props department modified it a bit to be a little bit closer to the angel-killing dagger that was used to kill Rachel, Castiel's lieutenant."

Somewhere in Heaven there is a storehouse of powerful supernatural weapons, the most common of which is the **ANGEL BLADE**, aka the angel-killing dagger. Although silver in color, it's unknown what alloy this weapon is made of, and it's unlikely that its original purpose was to kill angels, but during the war in Heaven, that becomes its primary use. However, the blade is equally efficient at killing Hellhounds—and, no doubt, humans, too. Heavenly power is imbued in the blade, allowing it to be used effectively by anyone, including demons and humans, as demonstrated when Dean uses one to kill Zachariah. The **ARCHANGEL BLADE** looks the same to mortal eyes, but it's been supercharged (presumably from being wielded by an archangel) and is capable of killing even these most powerful of angels. It is not, however, capable of killing an angel that's absorbed millions of souls, hence Castiel's resilience to its powers.

A rare modification of the angel blade is the **HEAVENLY BLADE**, which has been fine-tuned to kill powerful gods like the Fates. After their little misunderstanding over the sinking of the *Titanic*, Balthazar almost uses one of these golden daggers on Atropos, but the goddess talks her way out of that situation.

Despite their supernatural deadliness, the blades are the equivalent of mere knives next to rocket launchers in comparison to the more famous heavenly weapons, such as the **STAFF**

OF MOSES. The staff can control water, cover people in boils, and summon a plague of locusts, among other things. Don't let parlor tricks such as the staff's ability to transform into a snake fool you; this is a powerful weapon that is effective against angels in human vessels. Previously used by Moses in his display of dominance against the Egyptians, it is now in less potent pieces scattered throughout Heaven, thanks to Balthazar's failed get-souls-quick scheme (as documented in "The Third Man"). The rogue angel had it shattered into several parts so that they could be accessed whenever he needed them.

LOT'S SALT ROCK was used on humans when Lot's wife disobeyed the angels' order not to look back at Sodom, the doomed city her family was fleeing. Her eyes fell on the supercharged salt crystal and she was instantly transformed into a pillar of salt. Archangel Raphael's vessel, Donnie Finnerman, suffers the same demise when Balthazar saves Castiel from a smiting.

The name of **GABRIEL'S HORN OF TRUTH** says it all—when blown, it compels all who hear it to speak the truth. Then there's the **ARK OF THE COVENANT**, probably the most famous and most powerful of all heavenly weapons. Its true usage is unclear, but Castiel doesn't refute that it's in the

form of a gold box and that looking inside it will melt the faces off humans. Suffice it to say, it's the heavenly equivalent of a nuclear device—a nuke on supernatural steroids.

During the civil war in Heaven, Balthazar stole many of these famous items, weapons that even the Archangel Raphael feared. Balthazar turned the items over to his friend Castiel, who hid them away. Considering Castiel's current mental state, he's not likely to ever use them. It's even quite possible he's forgotten where they are . . .

Holy Smoke!

Holy Fire is a very effective weapon for fighting angels. Quite simply, it is Holy Oil set on fire. But Holy Oil is a rare substance and its composition and origins are unknown, although Castiel manages to obtain some in Jerusalem. A circle of Holy Fire will entrap an angel as surely as a Devil's Trap will hold a demon. Holy Fire can also be used to burn angels out of their vessels, or at least cause them to teleport to the nearest body of water.

ABOVE: Balthazar uses Lot's Salt Rock on fellow angel Raphael, turning his vessel into a literal pile of salt. TOP RIGHT: Lot's Salt Rock is one of the biblical weapons stolen from Heaven. ABOVE RIGHT: A piece of the Staff of Moses, severed into segments by Balthazar.

BEHIND THE SCENES

ABOVE LEFT: Lilith (Katherine Boecher) in her white dress right before she is killed by Sam in the season 4 finale, "Lucifer Rising." ABOVE CENTER: Crowley (Mark Sheppard) always dresses to impress in bespoke suits. ABOVE RIGHT: Julia Maxwell's Eve costume after she is killed by ingesting the phoenix ash (episode 619, "Mommy Dearest").

THE COSTUME DEPARTMENT

"*Supernatural* is a great show to design," says costume designer Diane Widas. Since *Supernatural* is set in the present with people who are often blue collar and rarely wealthy, Widas points out that "it's a fun challenge to make regular people look interesting." Of course, it's not all regular folk on the show; the costume department has had the opportunity to design clothes for clowns, dolls, faeries, and scarecrows, plus countless monsters and historical characters from various time periods.

But even costumes as plain as prison uniforms get special attention. When Gordon Walker was in jail in "Bad Day at Black Rock," the costume department chose a prison uniform that worked with the set. "We tried to make Gordon really fit into the prison by giving him the same-colored outfit as the background," Widas explains.

Likewise, Widas color-coordinated the Four Horsemen's attire with the legendary colors of their horses. "For Pestilence, I incorporated a little green into his costume. It's not like he's the green guy, but I tried to do it in a subtle enough way that if anybody knows the history and the mythology, they would know what we were trying to do."

The costume department often uses colors to reflect something about the story. For the alternate-reality portion of "What Is and What Should Never Be," Widas says, they "used brighter colors to help reflect happier times." Likewise, for "Dream a Little Dream of Me," she says, "the colors popped more in Dean's dream about Lisa; she was in sunshiny colors, making it all seem like everything was wonderful."

TOP LEFT: Sam and Dean's doctor outfits from season 5's "Changing Channels." TOP RIGHT: Jared Padalecki's "work" outfit from "Swap Meat" (episode 512).
ABOVE LEFT: Jensen Ackles' gym-teacher outfit (complete with plum-smuggling shorts) from episode 413, "After School Special." ABOVE CENTER: Continuity photo for Ackles' gym-teacher costume. ABOVE RIGHT: Misha Collin's grungy "Future Castiel" outfit from episode 504, "The End."

TOP LEFT: Ruby (Genevieve Padalecki) always liked to appear chic and cool whenever she reared her lovely but dangerous head. TOP CENTER: Jim Beaver's outfits as Bobby Singer were always utilitarian, practical, and well worn. TOP RIGHT: Becky Rosen's (Emily Perkins) wedding dress from the season 7 episode, "Season 7, Time for a Wedding!" ABOVE LEFT: Dean and Eliot Ness (Nicholas Lea) cut a dash while hunting the time lord Chronos in season 7's, "Time After Time." ABOVE CENTER: One of the terrifying clowns from episode 714, "Plucky Pennywhistle's Magical Menagerie." ABOVE RIGHT: Jensen Ackles' iconic lederhosen from season 4's "Monster Movie."

Possibly the greatest variety of colors in one scene can be found in the party sequence from "It's the Great Pumpkin, Sam Winchester." Instead of creating original Halloween costumes for all the teen extras in this and the crypt scene, most of the outfits were purchased from regular costume shops. "These days, kids buy their costumes as opposed to making them," Widas points out, "so most of the Halloween costumes were things we bought and augmented."

The prize for most impressive variety of costumes in one episode goes to Jared Padalecki and Jensen Ackles for their work in "Changing Channels." "There were a lot of changes for the boys, which is quite unusual for them. It was difficult from

a production standpoint because they had to send the actors back and forth to change a lot," Widas recalls. "I tried to make the things that were in the TV shows brighter and bolder even with the brothers' own clothing, and then, when they're in real time, I used the more muted colors we usually go for. Making them into the doctors and all that was pretty crazy fun."

Not as crazy as putting Dean in lederhosen in "Monster Movie," however. When asked about her favorite costume, there's one outfit that stands out even more for Widas. "One of my favorite things to do is period stuff, and making Jensen look like everybody's '80s high school gym coach with the little red shorts was totally fun."

TOP LEFT: Continuity photo for Faran Tahir's Osiris … TOP RIGHT: And the on-screen costume from episode 704, "Defending Your Life." ABOVE LEFT: When Dean and Sam travel back in time to the Old West, Dean is only too happy to embrace the period's clothing. ABOVE CENTER: Dean Winchester, a study in Old West Cool. ABOVE RIGHT: Sam is less than thrilled with the living conditions of the 1800s.

"Doing a Western episode is something that we always talked about," comments executive producer Bob Singer. But the question was, "How to do a Western in the *Supernatural* universe?" With the phoenix-ash storyline in 'Frontierland,' Singer says, "we finally found the right thing that would fit into the mythology for us to do a Western. It had a backstory to it because we used the whole Samuel Colt angle. We've gone back in time before, so it was not something that was totally out of left field for us; it felt organic."

Getting a storyline that worked was the first step to making a Western believable on *Supernatural*. Finding a location that would be convincing as an Old West town was the second step, and fortunately, a suitable background was readily available, thanks to the still-standing set from an old TV show called *Bordertown*. But the third and possibly most important step was making the characters *look* like they lived and breathed the Old West. Unlike Dean, no one from *Supernatural*'s costume department ran out to Wally's Western World for Western wear; they researched the real deal and made costumes that looked and felt authentic.

CHAPTER 7

ANCIENT EVIL

SEASON 7: THE STORY

"It is a new day on Earth and in Heaven. Rejoice!" With these words, the new God, Castiel, sets about cleaning up the old God's messes, starting with wiping out every angel that stood against Castiel in his war with the Archangel Raphael. On Earth, he smites errant religious leaders and bigots, eradicates the Ku Klux Klan, and heals lepers and the sick. Not necessarily bad things, but Sam and Dean believe Castiel is out of control, so they search for a way to stop him. What they don't know is that something is also very wrong with Castiel; something he absorbed from Purgatory is trying to break free of his human vessel . . .

Dean realizes that there is someone who can stop Castiel: Death. Crowley, who isn't too pleased with having Castiel as his new boss, provides Bobby and the Winchesters with a binding spell to summon the Horseman. Castiel arrives shortly after Death does, and Death warns the angel that the things inside him are Leviathan, creatures older than angels—and much more dangerous. Too drunk with power to listen, Castiel threatens to

kill Death. Dean demands that Death kill Castiel first, but the mutated angel removes Death's bindings, then flees. Annoyed by Castiel's arrogance, Death creates an eclipse so the portal to Purgatory can be reopened. Convincing Castiel to relinquish the souls he is containing is easier than expected when Dean and Sam find out the angel is losing control of his vessel and wants to get rid of the Leviathan inside him. Only, he can't.

When Castiel returns the monster souls to Purgatory, the Leviathan hold on. They take over Castiel's body and force it to walk into a lake. With an explosion of black goo, Castiel disintegrates, leaving just his trench coat behind as the Leviathan spread out into the United States through water supplies. Although he hasn't forgiven Castiel for tearing Sam's soul wall down, Dean is still hit hard by the death of his friend. Sam has troubles of his own to deal with; Lucifer is visiting him in hallucinations and trying to convince him that he's still in Hell, and that everything that has happened since Sam jumped into the pit has been the vivid dream of a tortured mind.

OPPOSITE: Sam and Dean's investigations will lead them into the path of the Leviathan, whether they like it or not … TOP LEFT: Dean summons Death in order to ask the Horseman's help in stopping Castiel from his misguided mission as the new Messiah. TOP RIGHT: Bobby starts to worry when Castiel appears to face off against Death. CENTER LEFT: Death and Castiel go face-to-face when the Horseman warns the delusional angel that he has unleashed something far more dangerous than souls from the very depths of Purgatory … CENTER RIGHT: Castiel can no longer contain the Leviathan in his rapidly decomposing human vessel … ABOVE LEFT: Sam can no longer tell the difference between nightmare and reality now that he constantly sees Lucifer wherever he is and hears the Devil in his head as well. ABOVE RIGHT: Dean tries to reason with a fragile Sam in order to keep his mind focused on the hunt for the Leviathan rather than letting Lucifer invade his thoughts.

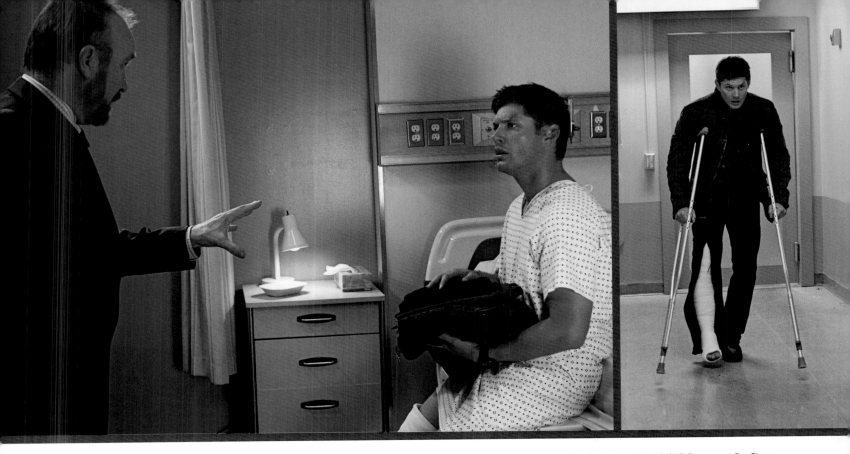

ABOVE LEFT: Bobby arrives at Sioux Falls General before Sam and Dean can be killed by the Leviathan, who are posing as hospital staff. ABOVE RIGHT: Dean must flee Sioux Falls General as fast as he can, despite being hindered by crutches and a broken leg, before the Leviathan catch up with him. OPPOSITE, TOP LEFT AND TOP RIGHT: Leviathan posing as Sam and Dean go on a ruthless killing spree in order to discredit the Winchesters and make them outlaws. OPPOSITE, CENTER: Forced to put his beloved car in storage after the Leviathan posing as him and Sam drove an identical one, Dean must deal with one junker after another … OPPOSITE, BOTTOM LEFT: Sam and Dean tussle with two witches (Buffy the Vampire Slayer alums James Marsters and Charisma Carpenter) in Prosperity, Indiana. OPPOSITE, BOTTOM RIGHT: Dean and Bobby ponder what to do about Sam's slipping grasp on reality thanks to his near-constant hallucinations of Lucifer.

Able to shapeshift into any human form they want with just one touch of their victim, the Leviathan quickly work their way into society. Sam and Dean's first encounter with their new foes does not go well, leaving Dean with a broken leg and Bobby's house burned to the ground. Even dropping a car on top of a Leviathan barely slows it down. Things soon go from very bad to worse when the Leviathan clone Sam and Dean and learn all their aliases, all their habits—literally everything about them. Then the clones go on a killing spree, which puts the Winchesters on the Most Wanted list of every law-enforcement agency across the country. Just in time, and by accident, Bobby discovers that Borax, a household cleaning product, burns the Leviathan like supernatural acid, and that beheading the Leviathan and keeping them from reattaching kills them. The boys eventually catch up with their clones and manage to decapitate them, ending the FBI's manhunt. But the Leviathan are still hunting them. At Bobby's urging, Sam and Dean turn to a friend of his, Frank Devereaux, for help, and the unstable but wily hunter gives them new IDs, wipes Sam's computer by completely destroying it, and—much to Dean's horror—makes them put the Winchester car in storage.

While they try to figure out how to actually kill the Leviathan, Sam and Dean battle a kitsune (creatures that feed on the brains of humans), the pagan god Osiris, a bickering pair of married witches, a ghost, and a plethora of demons. But even those hunts are complicated. The kitsune, Amy, was Sam's childhood friend, and when they were young she killed her own mother to protect him. So when Amy kills some lowlifes to save her sick kitsune son's life, Sam lets her go with the promise that she will only feed on corpses. Dean, however, figures once a monster, always a monster, so he ganks her behind Sam's back. Osiris preys on guilt, and he forces the ghost of Jo Harvelle to kill Dean because he feels responsible for her death, but Sam kills the Egyptian god, freeing Jo and saving Dean. Then Sam faces his most dangerous opponent yet: his number one fan, Becky! She slips him a love potion and they get *married*, confounding Dean, who has to team up with misfit hunter Garth to get to the root of the matter. It turns out a Crossroads Demon has been manipulating Becky, but she redeems herself (somewhat) by helping the Winchesters kill the demon. This leads to an encounter with Crowley, who tells the boys he's ordered all demons to leave them alone so that they'll be unencumbered to hunt down their mutual enemies, the Leviathan.

Under the guidance of their leader, billionaire Dick Roman, the Leviathan are planning something huge, but the hunters have no idea what. The first clue comes in the form of the new Turducken Slammer sandwiches at Biggerson's, a restaurant chain now owned by Roman Enterprises. A special additive to the meat is making people so hungry they'll eat anything—including other people! Ironically, this is an unexpected side effect, as the purpose of the additive is to make people fat and docile. The turducken program is scrapped, however, because Dick's golden rule states

TOP: Sam and Dean temporarily work with a unique hunter named Garth, with near-disastrous results! ABOVE LEFT: The Leviathan leader is disguised as billionaire businessman Dick Roman. ABOVE RIGHT: Sam and Dean are devastated when Bobby dies thanks to a fatal bullet wound from Dick Roman. RIGHT: As he travels closer to death, Bobby confronts memories of the past, including the time he shot and killed his cruel and abusive father.

TOP LEFT: *After Bobby's death, Dean and Sam distract themselves from their grief by dealing with cursed antiques …* TOP RIGHT: *A murderous vetala …*
ABOVE LEFT: *A deadly shojo …* ABOVE RIGHT: *And Sam's worst nightmare: killer clowns!*

that there should be no monsters on earth, and the cannibals are drawing way too much media attention. That's the good news. The bad news is that Dick captures Bobby. Sam and Dean rescue their friend, of course, but as they're racing away, Dick shoots Bobby in the head.

Then Bobby Singer does the unthinkable and dies.

After Bobby's death, Dean becomes obsessed with a series of numbers Bobby whispered to him and Sam before he passed away. With Frank's help, he figures out they're coordinates for a plot of land where the Leviathan are building something. The problem is, Dean still has no idea what. Complicating matters, Sam's Lucifer hallucinations are getting worse, and Dean wonders if he's going crazy himself, since he thinks Bobby's ghost might be haunting him. As much as he wants to focus on the Leviathan problem, the other things that go bump in the night keep getting in the way. The Winchesters take on more ghosts, demons, and various cursed objects, as well as vetala, the pagan god Chronos (with the time-traveling help of crime-fighting hero Eliot Ness), a shojo, and Sam's worst nightmare: killer clowns. They even have to fight Dean's

daughter. After a one-night stand with an Amazon results in a child with a supernatural growth spurt, Dean finds himself face-to-face with his monster offspring—who's been indoctrinated to kill her own father. Dean gives her a chance to walk away, but Sam kills her without hesitation, pointing out that Dean did the same with Amy. The brothers' rule is nonnegotiable: you kill the monster, plain and simple.

They still don't know how to kill Leviathan, however, and there's one more monster Sam can't kill—the one inside his head: Lucifer. A sleep-deprived Sam eventually gets in a car accident and winds up in a mental hospital. Desperate to help his brother, Dean tracks down the mysterious Emmanuel, a man said to be able to miraculously heal people. Emmanuel turns out to be an amnesia-riddled Castiel, who is otherwise very much alive and well. Smiting demons brings back his memories, but Castiel informs Dean that he can't fix Sam. Ashamed that Sam's condition is his fault, Castiel transfers the younger Winchester's damaged soul material into his own being as an act of contrition, leaving Sam once again in full charge of his mental faculties.

TOP LEFT: An amnesiac Castiel learns from Meg and Dean who—and what—he really is and all that has transpired since he was presumed dead. ABOVE RIGHT: Bobby's back, but as a ghost, and if he does not stop his mission for revenge against Dick Roman, he will become a vengeful spirit doomed for Hell. ABOVE LEFT: Sam and Dean take a well-deserved break before resuming their hunt for Dick Roman and the Leviathan.

For the first time since jumping into Hell, Sam is his sane old self again. Dean's not crazy, either: Bobby *was* haunting him—or, rather, he was haunting his old flask that Dean kept after his death. Bobby eventually gets control of his ghost abilities and shares with Sam and Dean what he knows about Dick Roman's plans. The Leviathan intend to cure diseases in humans in order to create the most perfect, plump, docile, and nutritious food source. Yet that doesn't explain why Dick's also been conducting archaeological digs all around the world. A computer hacker named Charlie who works for one of Dick Roman's many companies helps the Winchesters figure that mystery out. In the process, Sam and Dean intercept an ancient stone tablet being delivered to Dick and discover that it contains the actual Word of God. The brothers turn to a now-revived Castiel for help, but it is the new prophet Kevin Tran, a high school student who accidentally came into contact

with the stone tablet, who is able to read and translate what turns out to be an instruction manual for killing Leviathan. Because of Kevin's special status, Castiel commands two angels from his garrison to watch over the prophet.

The Leviathan kill the angels guarding Kevin and abduct him. Dick threatens Kevin's mother's life, so the frightened young prophet translates the tablet for the Leviathan leader. Now it's a race for Sam and Dean to obtain the ingredients for the Leviathan-killing weapon. The Alpha Vampire's blood is crucial, so Leviathan Edgar tries to kill the alpha, but Sam and Dean rescue him, and the alpha gratefully shares his blood. The King of Hell's blood is also needed, so Dick offers to make Canada a Leviathan-free demon playground in exchange for all demons permanently vacating America and Crowley agreeing to give the Winchesters fake blood. Crowley agrees, then double-crosses Dick and gives

TOP LEFT: Castiel awakens from his coma a changed—and pacifist—angel. TOP RIGHT: High school student Kevin Tran accidentally becomes a Prophet of the Lord and the only one able to translate the cuneiform writing on the tablet containing the Word of God. ABOVE LEFT: In order to defeat the Leviathan, the Winchesters need the blood of the Alpha Vampire ... ABOVE RIGHT: They need Crowley's blood as well. But can the King of Hell be trusted not to double-cross them?

his real blood to Sam and Dean. Castiel's blood is also required, and even though the angel is struggling with his own existential crisis and refuses to fight, he gives the Winchesters his blood for the weapon as well.

Meanwhile, Bobby's losing his ghostly sanity, too. He's so obsessed with getting revenge on his murderer, Dick Roman, that he possesses an innocent motel maid and nearly gets her killed. As a result he almost kills Sam, before snapping out of his rage and leaving the woman's body. Not wanting to become a vengeful spirit, Bobby insists Sam and Dean burn his flask, thereby banishing his spirit from Earth. The brothers agree, and bid Bobby a last farewell as his spirit is put to rest.

In order to kill the Leviathan, Sam and Dean pour the blood of the three fallen—Castiel, a fallen angel; Crowley, the ruler of fallen humanity; and the Alpha Vampire, the father of fallen beasts—onto the bone of a righteous mortal (in this case a nun

who was the very model of selflessness in life) and storm the Leviathan stronghold at SucroCorp—Dick Roman's latest corporation. Driving the newly recommissioned Impala, Meg creates a distraction for the Winchesters, all the while hoping to convince Castiel to kill Crowley on her behalf. Meanwhile, Sam rescues Kevin, while Dean and Castiel locate Dick. Dean stabs the Leviathan leader with the bone, and Dick Roman explodes. However, it doesn't erase the Leviathan leader from existence; it merely sends him back to Purgatory. Crowley arrives and informs Sam that he put a spell on his blood so that in addition to the Leviathan being sent back to Purgatory, Dean and Castiel are sucked in as well. Crowley takes Kevin and Meg and disappears, leaving Sam alone to find his brother and Castiel.

But both Dean and Castiel are now in Purgatory, surrounded by countless monster souls intent on ripping the heroes to shreds ...

TOP: The new, gentler Castiel tries to make amends to the Winchesters with sandwiches—and a vial of his blood to help defeat the Leviathan. ABOVE LEFT: Three vials of blood and the bone of a pious nun are the ingredients necessary to defeat Dick Roman ... ABOVE RIGHT: But when combined, the results are uncustomarily anticlimactic for Dean and Sam. OPPOSITE, TOP: Armed with Borax and their supernatural bone, the Winchesters and Castiel prepare to face off against Dick Roman and his fellow Leviathan. OPPOSITE, BOTTOM: Meg provides the Winchesters with a distraction so they can reach Dick Roman without being discovered.

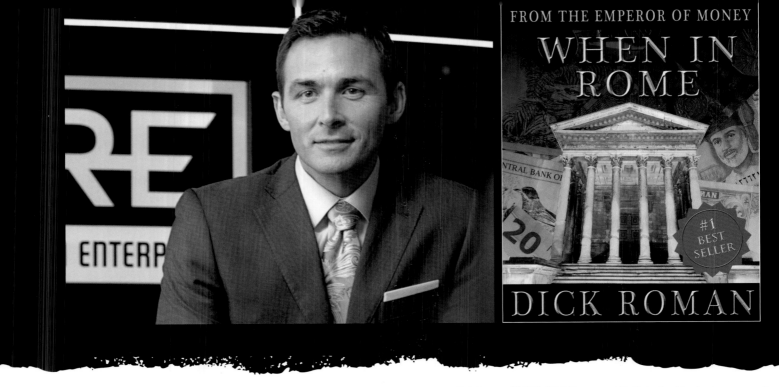

ABOVE LEFT: The leader of the Leviathan cleverly disguised himself as innovative businessman Dick Roman. ABOVE RIGHT: The cover of Dick's best-selling business manual.

LEVIATHAN AMONG US

L ong before God created angels and humans, he made the first beasts: the Leviathan. Clever and nearly invulnerable, they had a bad habit of eating everything God subsequently created. They even killed angels, leading God to create a Purgatory in which to lock the Leviathan away.

That is, until Castiel inadvertently let them back into the world.

Leviathan are the greatest threat to humanity since, well . . . ever. In their natural state they appear as a black goo that can travel through fluids, but once they possess a human body they are able to shapeshift into any other human they touch, stealing their knowledge and personality quirks in the process. Although Leviathan appear indistinguishable from humans, their large, sharp tooth–filled mouths can expand to engulf a person's head. They have super strength and regenerate quickly from wounds. At first, Sam and Dean have no idea how to stop them—nor does anybody else.

Leviathan can actually stop other Leviathan. There is a hierarchy to their society, it transpires, and underlings are often eaten if they displease their superiors. A particularly cruel punishment, known as bibbing, consists of Leviathan being forced to eat themselves. But there's little chance of the Leviathan eating each other into extinction, not when there are billions of humans ripe for the picking.

By happenstance, Bobby discovers that Borax is toxic to Leviathan. It doesn't kill them, though; it only slows them down. Still, splashing them with it provides enough time to escape or to behead them. Of course, beheading Leviathan is only a temporary solution, but put enough distance between the head and the body and the beast will effectively be neutralized.

Sam and Dean don't have the time to behead the Leviathan one by one, because their leader, Dick Roman, has big plans for the human race, and he's already started to implement them. The Leviathan prefer their cattle to be big, fat, stupid, slow, and perfectly healthy, so they are planning to cure major human diseases like cancer, weed out the inferior, damaged, or overly intelligent, and keep everyone so drugged up that they won't complain about being eaten. As a beneficial side effect, the new and improved humans will be poisonous to all other monsters, effectively wiping out the competition.

Which is why the Alpha Vampire and the King of Hell both help the Winchesters put together a weapon to kill Dick. An ancient tablet inscribed with the Word of God reveals that the only thing that kills Leviathan is a righteous human bone washed in the blood of "three of the fallen." Sam and Dean steal a dead nun's bone and cover it in the mixed bloods of the Alpha Vampire, Crowley, and Castiel. Then Dean uses it to destroy Dick Roman. Although he and Castiel get sucked into Purgatory along with the Leviathan, it's still a victory for humankind. With the head of their ancient hierarchal structure severed, the Leviathan will be confused and fragmented. Without a master plan, they're just more monsters to be hunted. But unless Sam and Dean are reunited, hunting and beheading the Leviathan could take a long, long time . . .

JAMES PATRICK STUART

J ames Patrick Stuart explains how he approached the role of head Leviathan Dick Roman. "The idea of Dick being a sort of motivational speaker gone horribly wrong really appealed to the producers," he says. "It just worked; I really clicked with them." Even so, the producers were cagey about whether the role would be ongoing. "They didn't indicate that the character would be recurring," Stuart says, "but it was sort of self-evident. In my first episode we clearly establish that there's something that Dick Roman wanted, and they needed to answer that question eventually.

I just had to fill in the blanks with my own emotional choices because they wanted to keep the secrets hidden; they keep their cards close to their chests."

Stuart had a lot of fun making those choices for his character. "Dick Roman gets great joy out of pretending to be a human, so it was an opportunity for me to just really exploit/borrow from/completely steal/plagiarize my favorite baddies of all time. My feeling has been that Dick Roman is observing as

many people as he can and taking their personality traits. I mean, it makes sense to me that he would borrow, because Leviathan is the ultimate plagiarist; he just takes your work for himself. For me that was a real thrill. This was my chance to be the shark from *Jaws,* because when I was growing up, while the rest of the kids were rooting for the heroes, I was always on the shark's side."

SECTION C
SPECIAL FEATURE:
A DAY IN THE LIFE
OF A WAR VETERAN
LIFE AFTER IRAQ
& HOW THEY COPE

The Indianapolis Sun

WEATHER TODAY
HI 63° LO 49°
PARTLY CLOUDY
LIGHT SHOWERS
DETAILS P.5

WWW.INDIANAPOLISSUN.COM · THE VOICE OF THE PEOPLE, THE NEWS OF THE WORLD · DECEMBER 5TH, 2010

Corporate Merger Worth 36.2 Million

Richard Roman Enterprises Buys Asian Telecommunications Giant, Share Prices Rocket

survivors, but are not having any luck." He went on to say.

Among those on the plane were up to 10 government workers, including journalists, and federal police officers. At least 4 doctors and many many families. They also estimate at least 25 children and 35 mothers. Flight Attendant Amanda Walker, was lost as well. Amanda had recently survived another crash. Veteran Pilot Captain Chuck Lambert survived the previous crash as well. Homeland security has ruled out terrorism as a cause of this crash.

"We are still looking into the exact mechanics, and will know more as we uncover more evidence from the crash site, however, this crash had nothing to do international affairs." Paul Howard, Assistant Chief of Homeland Security stated. Authorities are still piecing together exactly what happened on that plane, and hopefully can give families some sort of answer. An exact list of the deceased will be published. If anyone has any information, please contact United Brittania, the information desk at Indianapolis International or Pittsburgh International Airport.

Pittsburgh PA - A tragic plane crash today involving Flight 424 United Britannia Airlines leaves no survivors. All ninety-nine passengers and eight United Britannia airline workers have been declared dead. The flight was en route from Indianapolis International Airport to Pittsburgh International Airport. It departed at 8:08 a.m. Eastern Standard Time and was scheduled to arrive in Pittsburgh at 12:39 p.m. Experts say the flight started to go down forty minutes in, due to an unknown cause, however crashed outside of Pittsburgh. The flight was going down the majority of the time. This is the second crash for United Britannia Airlines this year. The airline is absolutely devastated. Officials state the cause of the crash is mechanical failure.

"So far we can gather this tragedy is due to mechanical failure. We are still unclear on how the cabin depressurized." One Pittsburgh official stated. The cockpit voice recorder gives clues to passengers screaming, panicked, and then an unidentifiable howl.

"We are using our best resources to determine what that noise actually

survivors, but are not having any luck." He went on to say.

Among those on the plane were up to 10 government workers, including journalists, and federal police officers. At least 4 doctors and many many families. They also estimate at least 25 children and 35 mothers. Flight Attendant Amanda Walker, was lost as well. Amanda had recently survived another crash. Veteran Pilot Captain Chuck Lambert survived the previous crash as well. Homeland security has ruled out terrorism as a cause of this crash.

"We are still looking into the exact mechanics, and will know more as we uncover more evidence from the crash site, however, this crash had nothing to do international affairs." Paul Howard, Assistant Chief of Homeland Security stated. Authorities are still piecing together exactly what happened on that plane, and hopefully can give families some sort of answer. An exact list of the deceased will be published. If anyone has any information, please contact United Brittania, the information desk at Indianapolis International or Pittsburgh International Airport.

US Daily Monitor ONLINE

THE NATION'S BEST ONLINE NEWS SOURCE   TODAY'S TOP STORIES

The Roman Empire Expands

Corporate Executive & Entrepreneur Becomes Bestselling Author

Los Angeles - Much of financial planning fails to account for the investor's human capital, and how that interacts with financial capital. Dick Roman address the issue in depth in a recent CFA Institute Monograph, Lifetime Financial Advice: Human Capital, Asset Allocation, and Insurance.

Human capital, in the context of the monograph, is simply the present value of a person's future earnings. When the investor is young, human capital likely far exceeds financial capital. As retirement approaches, financial capital needs to be able to replace the income as human capital dwindles. Much of financial planning fails to account for the investor's human capital, and how that interacts with financial capital. Dick Roman address the issue in depth in a recent CFA Institute Monograph, Lifetime Financial Advice: Human Capital, Asset Allocation, and Insurance.

FROM THE EMPEROR OF MONEY
WHEN IN ROME
#1 BEST SELLER
DICK ROMAN

REVIEWS: M. A. Liu on Roman's new book

Financial Planning: What you need to know

98 Comments

1 of 1   04/08/11 4:29pm

Limited time only!
NEW!
Pepperjack
Turducken Slammer!

NOW ONLY
$4.99

SIZZLIN' GRILL & BAR
BIGGERSON'S
All You Can Eat! · *Family Restaurant*

BR **BICKLEBEE REALTY**
RESIDENTIAL & COMMERCIAL

Search [COMMERCIAL PROPERTY 🔍]

Market News | Commercial Listings | Residential Listings | Mortgage Calculator

Joyce Bicklebee

Welcome to Bicklebee Realty! I'm here to help you sell your home, or find the perfect property for your needs, whether it's residential or commercial. With over 20 years experience in the Real Estate Market, I'm one of Portland's top realtors. I specialize in National and International property listings, with a strong sales record in all areas. Contact us today!

Featured Listings: 340856346
COMMERCIAL PROPERTY FOR SALE

PRIME RETAIL SPACE IN SHOPPING DISTRICT

LISTING DETAILS

LIST PRICE: $365,000
SQ': 1,205
PARKING: 2
YEAR BUILT: 2003
CONST: CONCRETE
LANDSCAPING: NO
LOADING: AT REAR
OFFICE SPACE: YES
WAREHOUSE: NONE
SECURITY: CONTRACT
ADDITIONAL UNITS: NO

A great opportunity for a retail / warehouse business development. Quality construction, with excellent location.

TOP, LEFT AND RIGHT: U.S. publications spotlighting Dick Roman's meteoric rise to success, proof that the Leviathan integrated themselves nearly flawlessly into human culture. ABOVE LEFT: The Turducken Slammer was a delicious but less-than-successful experiment by the Leviathan to fatten up humans for easy slaughter. CENTER AND ABOVE RIGHT: Two more Leviathan that invaded human society were real estate mogul Joyce Bicklebee and her hapless assistant George.

ABOVE: Bobby reminds Dean and Sam that he is always there for the Winchesters and will help them hunt down and kill Lilith.

LOSING BOBBY SINGER

Bobby Singer's life story has been punctuated by loss. He lost his wife when she was possessed by a demon. At that time he knew nothing about demons; he thought the woman he loved was already dead when he stabbed the monster she'd become. He was wrong. If he'd known about salt, holy water, Devil's Traps, and exorcisms, he could have saved her. He might have lost his sanity as well if Rufus Turner hadn't come along, rescuing Bobby from the demon that possessed his wife, then teaching him how to channel his grief and rage into becoming a hunter.

Flash-forward over twenty years later, and Bobby once again finds himself stabbing a person who has been possessed by a demon; only, this time, it's to save a loved one from himself. Bobby's the one possessed, and the demon inside him is trying to make him kill his surrogate son, Dean Winchester. Instead, he turns the demon-killing knife on himself. He doesn't die, but he does lose the use of his legs.

Bobby gets the use of his legs back eventually, though—and all it costs him is his soul. Crossroads Demon Crowley claims

he's just taking Bobby's soul on loan (in order to work the magic of the deal that locates Death, the leg usage being merely a bonus rider), but Bobby should have known better than to trust a demon. Thanks to some devilishly worded fine print, for all intents and purposes, Bobby's soul is lost to him.

With nothing else to lose, Bobby uses a handgun to take on Lucifer, who is now occupying Sam Winchester. The bullets merely irritate the fallen archangel, so he casually snaps Bobby's neck. For a brief moment, Bobby loses his life. Castiel resurrects him minutes later, however, but in the interim Bobby lost one of his surrogate sons, Sam, who sacrificed himself to stop the Apocalypse.

Castiel rescues Sam from Hell, but Bobby's fears about his crossroads deal are confirmed when Crowley admits he "just can't" give Bobby back his soul. But Bobby will be damned if he'll let a demon get the better of him. He researches everything there is to know about demons and discovers that if you can learn their human name and track down their remains, you can burn their bones just like any other pesky spirit's. The

TOP LEFT: A pensive Bobby waits to see what Sam will be like once his soul is restored. TOP RIGHT: A demon-possessed Bobby is about to surprise Dean in the worst way possible. ABOVE LEFT: A wheelchair-bound Bobby prepares to make a deal with Crowley for the use of his legs back. ABOVE RIGHT: A season 6 publicity image of Jensen Ackles, Jim Beaver, and Jared Padalecki.

threat of losing his bones is enough to make Crowley tear up Bobby's contract. He even generously allows Bobby to retain the use of his legs.

On the trail of the Mother of All Monsters months later, Bobby hits the road with the Winchester brothers and winds up on a case with his old hunting partner, Rufus. They argue over the incident that drove them apart, but while Rufus refuses to forgive Bobby, it's clear their friendship isn't a total loss after all. To his horror, Bobby loses control of his body to the Khan worm parasite and stabs Rufus to death.

With everything he's been through, Bobby no doubt expected to be eaten by a monster someday, but he loses his life to a regular bullet. At least he goes out with a bang: the bang

of a bullet shot from Dick Roman's antique revolver.

Yet, even in death Bobby is not willing to lose everything. He hangs on to his life with Sam and Dean, haunting his old flask, which Dean, devastated by Bobby's death, now carries around as a keepsake. Bobby wants to remain their father figure and keep them safe, but the problem with ghosts who are the product of violent deaths is that they tend to focus on the people who murdered them. The desire to kill Dick Roman is an itch Bobby can't scratch without turning into a vengeful spirit. Knowing his ghostly fate is sealed, he insists Sam and Dean burn the flask, thereby banishing him before he loses himself. One last good-bye, and Bobby is gone from the Winchesters' lives forever . . .

JIM BEAVER

When I got the offer to do my first episode of *Supernatural*," Jim Beaver recalls, "I had just been killed off on *Deadwood*, so I was pretty much under the impression that I would never work again, because that's what actors do when they lose a job; they figure that's it, the gravy train has run out. I was pleased to get the gig on *Supernatural*, but my impression was that it was a one-shot deal and that was the extent of it." Never did he imagine that he'd return for over *fifty* episodes.

In fact, even after he finished the first episode, Beaver had no reason to believe he'd be coming back. "I didn't have any particular feel at all that there would be anything recurring with the character," he says. "There was a lot of encouragement from the crew that because they hadn't killed me off I might be back, but almost every show you do, they say, 'Well, possibly we'll have you back,' and 99 percent of the time that doesn't mean anything, so it didn't mean much to me on *Supernatural,* either. I was pleasantly surprised to end up back for the very next episode! Then, by the third episode, it began to feel like, 'Oh, this may actually go somewhere.' But all through the second season, I didn't have much feeling that Bobby was going to be a big thing. I just thought, 'Every once in a while, they'll show up in South Dakota and need a place to stay and it'll be

convenient to have Bobby there.' Once I got to the end of season 2, with the Devil's Gate finale, I knew, 'Oh, okay, I'm really going to be a part of this show.' Still, my experience with acting in television is that you never count on anything, and even when you've got something that you're clearly a major part of, stories sometimes take strange turns—as we discover in 'Death's Door.'"

Despite dying in that episode, Beaver says it's one of his favorites. "'Death's Door' and 'Weekend At Bobby's' were really wonderful experiences for me, because as a guest star on the show it's extremely rare in that position to get to carry entire episodes and to be in almost every scene, so those are particular favorites for that reason. I also have special fondness for 'Dead Men Don't Wear Plaid' because I got to explore some of Bobby's backstory. That was a very difficult episode emotionally because it had a lot of resonances to my own life. Carrie Anne Fleming (who played Karen Singer) really helped me through that episode and gave me a great deal that I think a lot of other performers wouldn't have been able to. It was a rich and touching drama, and I like rich and touching drama. I like the funny stuff and I like the action stuff, but the ones that really grab me are the ones where we get to see the human heart in all its pain and glory; those episodes are the most enjoyable and most memorable for me."

ABOVE: Every detail of each set is painstakingly taken into account, from Dean's take-out container to the Tiki Motel signage in season 7's "Plucky Pennywhistle's Magical Menagerie." OPPOSITE, TOP: An aged and weather-beaten sign from episode 522, "Swan Song." OPPOSITE, BOTTOM: The cover to one of Dean's beloved porn magazines, Busty Asian Beauties.

THE ART DEPARTMENT—GRAPHIC DESIGN

"With *Supernatural*, I feel like we're making a feature film with every episode," comments graphic designer Lee-Anne Elaschuk. "I think over the years, instead of it becoming easier, in a lot of ways it's become more challenging in the sense that our viewers expect more, we expect more, and probably our directors do as well. From the art department point of view, I think we've raised the bar as high as we can. We certainly put a lot of effort into everything we do, and I think the episodes look great, so it's very rewarding."

The work the art department puts in doesn't go unnoticed—not by the fans, not by the rest of the crew, and certainly not by the showrunners. "They do not miss a beat!" exclaims executive producer Sera Gamble. For example, she says, "the creamer cups [from "Survival of the Fittest"] are adorable."

Putting SucroCorp labels on the creamers was a necessary part of the visual storytelling, and production designer Jerry

Wanek emphasizes that there's always a reason for what they do. "Like in the episode with Fate, we have E.J. Smith Travel because Edward John Smith was the captain of the *Titanic*, and we have an iceberg on the label of the beer that you see in the opening," Wanek points out. "We play around with a lot of things like that, but if something isn't cohesive with the style of what we're trying to do, it gets thrown out. For us, it's not about putting something in there to be cool—I don't think that's good storytelling, I don't think that's good design. For me, it's really important that you don't see something that makes you stop and go, 'What was that?'"

At least not the first time through the episode. After all, in the beginning of "My Heart Will Go On," you don't know it's about the *Titanic* yet, so you're not going to fixate on the fact that there happens to be an iceberg on the label. But during repeated viewings, it can be a lot of fun to look for all the little

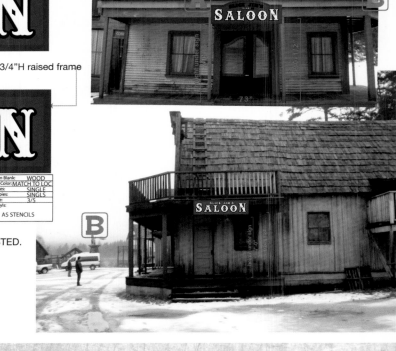

A 1-1/2"W X 3/4"H raised frame

SLICK JIM'S
SUNRISE
SALOON

B 1-1/2"W X 3/4"H raised frame

76"W X 21"H

SLICK JIM'S
SALOON

SEE PAINT AGING REFERENCE

FERNANDO:
PLEASE MAKE PAPER TEMPLATES FOR
SIGN BLANK & STENCILS FOR HAND PAINTING IF REQUESTED.

Sign Blank:	WOOD
BG Color:	MATCH TO LOC
Sides:	SINGLE
Copies:	SINGLS
Age:	3/5
Vinyls:	
	AS STENCILS

SUPERNATURAL	EP# 617
	SET# 6
	1
Mike Rohl	

DISTRIBUTION LIST	
ART DEPT.	X1
CONST.COORDINATOR	X5
CONSTRUCTION X	X5
PAINT COORDINATOR	X2
PAINT	X2
VINYL	X1
SET DEC	X1
PROPS	
COSTUMES	
TRANSPO	
VFx	

DIR. Ext. MAIN STREET
DATE: D1 TUE. JAN.25
DWG NAME: EXT. SALOON SIGNAGE
DRAWN BY: M.- A. LIU

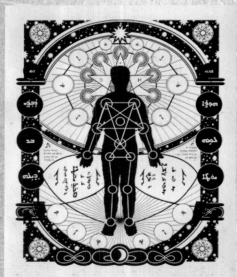

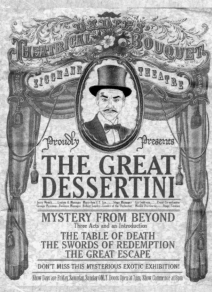

THE GREAT
DESSERTINI

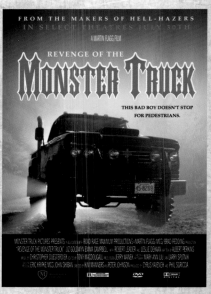

FROM THE MAKERS OF HELL-HAZERS
REVENGE OF THE
MONSTER TRUCK

TOP: Details covering everything from the dimensions and precise placement of the Slick Jim's Saloon signs to the color and texture of the aging paint on the saloon's exterior are all worked out in advance by the designers in the art department (from episode 618, "Frontierland"). ABOVE: Three more examples of the varied graphic needs include a spell-book page, an old flyer advertising a magic act, and a movie poster. RIGHT: The Honey Wagon Bar signage from episode 414, "Sex and Violence."

Honey Wagon
BAR

02A1-37N

CORONER

STATE OF MICHIGAN
CORONER

412-M-26
ISSUED: 09/08 EXPIRES: 09/12

021

10145-25A21N001-02-A1

WAYNE COUNTY CORONER'S OFFICE

DEPARTMENT OF THE CORONER
WAYNE COUNTY, MI

SECURITY
LEVEL 4
MAIN BLDG.

COUNTY MORGUE

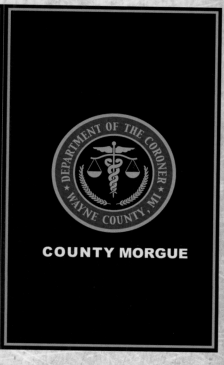

DEPARTMENT OF THE CORONER
WAYNE COUNTY, MI

COUNTY MORGUE

HEALTH INSPECTOR

THE SEAL OF THE STATE OF WASHINGTON
1889

D. Birk

WASHINGTON STATE DEPARTMENT OF HEALTH

DEPARTMENT of INVESTIGATION

AUTHENTIC PHOTOGRAPH / ID9015-47

FBI

DEPARTMENT OF JUSTICE
FEDERAL BUREAU OF INVESTIGATION

THIS CERTIFIES THAT THE SIGNATURE
AND PHOTOGRAPH ARE AUTHENTIC

SPECIAL AGENT _____

THE FEDERAL BUREAU OF JUSTICE
UNITED STATES DEPARTMENT OF INVESTIGATION

SHERWOOD POLICE DEPARTMENT
Investigations

POLICE

SHERWOOD POLICE DEPT.

NAME: E_____
LICENSE: 450GH0-23

ISSUED: 07.12.06

EXPIRES: 09.01.10

10145-25A21N001-02-A1

NUMBER 007 CODE 001X

DEPARTMENT of INVESTIGATION

AUTHENTIC PHOTOGRAPH / ID9015-47

FBI

DEPARTMENT OF JUSTICE
FEDERAL BUREAU OF INVESTIGATION

THIS CERTIFIES THAT THE SIGNATURE
AND PHOTOGRAPH ARE AUTHENTIC

SPECIAL AGENT _____

THE FEDERAL BUREAU OF JUSTICE
UNITED STATES DEPARTMENT OF INVESTIGATION

THIS PAGE: A bevy of Dean and Sam's fake IDs from past seasons.

555

DL 00756 632 DMV# 01
D.O.B. 12/16/1974 Sex M
Class C**** Eyes BRN
Conditions * Height 5'-11"
Restrictions *21
Issued 10/01/2004
Expiry 10/01/2010

3123 HOUSET STREET
PITTSBURG PA 15122

Pennsylvania DRIVERS LICENSE

DL

ABOVE: Shrimp-chips packaging for the Japanese game show segment of season 5's "Changing Channels." OPPOSITE, TOP LEFT: Bobby and Ellen pose in front of their alternate-reality scrap-yard sign in season 6's "My Heart Will Go On." OPPOSITE, CENTER LEFT: The real scrap-yard sign, with just Bobby, after Balthazar restores the timeline. OPPOSITE, TOP RIGHT: A Biggerson's menu promises the delicious rewards of their new Turducken Slammer sandwich. OPPOSITE, BOTTOM: The Johnny Mac's diner menu from episode 401, "Lazarus Rising."

things that the art department included. For example, the saloon in "Frontierland" is called Slick Jim's, which graphic designer Mary-Ann Liu says she named after co–executive producer Jim Michaels. "We've all been in it in some way," Wanek admits. "I was a dead person at one point, I was in an obituary, and then one time my name was on Dean's ID—things like that. Pretty much any given town, label, or name of a motel is game anytime someone comes up with something or wants to put in an ancestor or a relative. A lot of times the writers will also do stuff like that."

Sometimes there's stuff that the viewers will never see, but the graphic designers include anyway for themselves and the cast. "We always put a few little things in, like on menus," Liu says. "We'll put a funny name for a food item that Jensen and Jared would pick up on, but those are never seen by the camera. I'm really careful about that because the focus should not be on that." On the flipside, when the camera's

definitely going to pick things up, Liu is careful to make sure things look authentic. For instance, she says, "one of my favorite sets is the game show one in 'Changing Channels.' I really love using different languages in a set because visually it's different. For the 'Nutcracker' sign, I went through a computer translation, then I went through professional Japanese translators, then I had it proofed by our art director's Japanese friend. I go through as much as I need to in order to make sure the language is proper. If you don't, your credibility's gone instantly."

From creamer-cup labels to beer-bottle labels, from Wild West town signage to Japanese game show signage, there's never a dull moment in the art department. "My favorite thing about working on *Supernatural* is the way every episode is so unique," comments Elaschuk. "Every time you pick up a *Supernatural* script, you don't know what it's going to be about; they're all so different, so fresh. That is incredibly rewarding."

Breakfast

BACON 'N EGGS
$3.49
2 eggs any style
with toast, bacon
served with coffee

Lunch

BOB'S BEEF CHILLI
only **$4.29**
a local favorite
served over rice

Dinner

FISH & CHIPS PLATTER
breaded fish fillet
with french fries and salad
$6.29

$3.49 WE
L♥VE
WAFFLES!
3 waffles served with
hot fruit topping

HOT FRESH
COFFEE
FREE REFILLS!

Johnny Mac's

THE WORD ON SEASON 8

After doing a great job as showrunner on seasons 6 and 7, executive producer Sera Gamble decided to leave the show to pursue new projects. But she didn't leave the new showrunner, executive producer Jeremy Carver, in the lurch; she helped him and co-showrunner Bob Singer plan ahead. "As we were rounding on the end of season 7 and talking about the Word of God with Kevin Tran translating and what that could mean, and talking about Crowley stepping out of the shadows to play a bigger part in the finale, Bob and I had a lot of discussions about avenues that things like that could lead to in season 8," Gamble says. "I felt that my job was to propose different possibilities and then leave it in the hands of Bob and Jeremy for season 8."

There could be any number of tablets out there—the Word of God could be endless—as could the story ideas derived from it. "Crowley has Kevin, and what Kevin can read on the tablets leads to what is basically the mythology of season 8," Singer sums up. "We are going to put the

boys on a quest. It's not necessarily to save the world, but it is a quest."

Which means that the boys will of course be back together in season 8. "Oh, absolutely," Singer says. "At the end of season 7, Dean goes to Purgatory and Sam, as Crowley says, is left well and truly alone; but we're going to pick season 8 up a little bit down the line, and the guys are going to approach this year with different attitudes: Sam sees an end to this life, he sees himself getting out of it, whereas Dean, having been in Purgatory and having had to fight his way out, appreciated the purity of it. There was no artifice down there; it was just kill or be killed. So their attitudes going into season 8 are quite a bit different in terms of how they see themselves in the long run."

What exactly that means for the Winchester brothers and their relationship remains to be seen, but Jared Padalecki is looking forward to finding out. "We'll just keep on going in this crazy world, wherever it goes."

OPPOSITE AND TOP: Sam and Dean face an uncertain future with Dean trapped in Purgatory and Sam on his own ... ABOVE LEFT: There could be more than one tablet with the Word of God that the Winchesters must find—and that Crowley wants. ABOVE CENTER: Crowley has emerged as the big villain of season 8, and one the Winchesters will have a hard time defeating. ABOVE RIGHT: What role will Castiel play in the Winchesters' future? And what is the angel's own fate? LEFT: Once Sam and Dean are reunited, what will their dynamic be going forward, and will they be on the same path?

RETURNING CHARACTERS

Now that the head of the Leviathan has been figuratively cut off, will we be seeing them much, if at all, in season 8? "When leaving that storyline, the idea was that they were leaderless but still around us," notes executive producer Bob Singer, "so if somebody pitches a Leviathan story that sounds good, we have that option available to us." Which is essentially how they feel about all creatures and characters, although Singer did add, "We're not going to deal so much with Purgatory." Once Dean gets out of Purgatory, there's little chance it will be a pivotal story point anytime soon.

It's obvious, of course, that Dean will get out of Purgatory pretty quickly, but will Castiel get left behind, or will he be back with the boys in season 8? "Oh, we plan on using Castiel," Singer says. "Absolutely!" Things aren't so certain, however, with the beloved character Bobby. "I don't know if we will see him in season 8," Singer admits, "but if he does come back, it will be in flashbacks and things like that."

With *Supernatural*, it's possible to bring literally any character back. In fact, aside from the writers needing to find the right story vehicles, the only thing standing in the way of bringing certain characters back is the actors' schedules. Like Frank Devereaux, for instance, whose return relies more on Kevin McNally's availability than on how much blood was in Frank's trailer. And then, of course, there's John Winchester . . .

"The biggest one is John Winchester," producer Daniel Loflin agrees. "That's such an interesting situation, too, because every time we need John Winchester to do something in an episode, we try to find a way to not use that as a crutch. We try to find some other way around it, because we have characters come back from the dead all the time, but with John Winchester it seems like we're using that as a challenge to say, 'No, when some characters die, they actually die for good.' It's like, all the time, I wish I could speak to my [deceased] grandmother, but I can't; I can only just imagine what she'd say. I can't really talk to her,

OPPOSITE AND THIS PAGE: While Dean and Sam will definitely be back, what about the rest of the iconic players in the Winchester pantheon?

ABOVE LEFT: Jo Harvelle showed up in season 7 as a ghost, but now that she has been allowed to rest in peace, who will show up as a spirit in season 8?
ABOVE RIGHT: Crowley's plans for the demon Meg are unknown, even to her, and will she live to survive the season, or will we see her demise for good?

and I can't really get any kind of closure from her, and I feel like the Winchesters need a figure like that, too. It actually helps us with the drama because it challenges us to make the stories seem more true to life. John is obviously the best choice for that. Then, on top of that, Jeffrey Dean Morgan is difficult to get." Despite his busy work schedule, Morgan says, "I'm hoping I make another appearance. I'm not sure how or why, but we'll see. I will always have a soft place in my heart for those guys, and I think there were a lot of unresolved questions with John and the boys, so I've got my fingers crossed. There's always the future . . ."

Mary Winchester, on the other hand, has been back several times since her death. Yet, after her first return as a ghost, she's never truly been herself. Of course, actress Samantha Smith is happy to come back every time, regardless of whether she gets to continue Mary's true storyline or come back as an illusion. Smith keeps up with the show, and she says, "They have kept me guessing the whole time. I don't see where it's going. Even being involved with the show, I have no idea what's coming.

They always surprise me, so I'm dying to know what's next for Mary as well."

Like Sam and Dean, Jo Harvelle lost her father, and actress Alona Tal muses, "I can believe that when Jo and her mom got to Heaven that they got to be with her dad. Maybe the writers will do a storyline about her dad sharing something with the boys about a hunt he did with their father."

Another character who could be a treasure trove of hunting knowledge would be Samuel Colt, and actor Sam Hennings thinks it'd be a wonderful idea to bring him back. "I know they were happy with the results of my incarnation of Samuel Colt and the relationship that Jared and I had on-screen, so I hope that they would consider bringing me back," Hennings says. "If they do, it'll be great fun. I would love them to bring Samuel Colt to 2012. Can you imagine a guy like Samuel Colt getting transported from the 1860s into 2012 and have to look around at flat-screen TVs, telephones, and all that stuff? And then have to fight at the same time? That kind of stuff is fun to do!"

TOP, LEFT AND RIGHT: With a little good luck, the Ghostfacers will hopefully be back in season 8 to cause more mayhem and aggravation for Dean and Sam. ABOVE LEFT: The Alpha Vampire has promised retribution on the Winchesters, so will he be back to cause more trouble in season 8? ABOVE RIGHT: Have we seen the last of expert computer hacker Charlie, or will she return to help the Winchesters hunt down the rest of the Leviathan?

A dead hunter who's less likely to show up is Gordon Walker, who got turned into a vampire and then decapitated by Sam. "I would love him to come back," says creator Eric Kripke. "We could always bring him back as a ghost." Carrying his head in his hand? "Yeah! That'd be cool." Jensen Ackles and Jared Padalecki would love to have him back, too. "I thought Sterling Brown was a great addition to the show," Ackles says. "He did a great job," Padalecki concurs. "He's a lot of fun to have around."

Speaking of characters who are fun to have around, who wouldn't love to see the Ghostfacers return? "I hope to bring them back when the story's right for them," Kripke says. "We talk about that, for sure," Singer adds. "If we can find a place for them in season 8, we'll bring them back—we love the Ghostfacers!" You can count on the actors returning with great enthusiasm. "Any time that the *Supernatural* family welcomes us back, we're all ready to drop everything," Brittany Ishibashi (Maggie Zeddmore) assures us. "All of us were like, 'This is the

most fun we've ever had working! We're getting paid for this?' It's really like the best time you could ever have working." Executive producer Phil Sgriccia, who directed "Ghostfacers," feels the same way. "They're so much fun to work with; we're laughing every day at work," he says. "I'd love to have them back," states Ackles. "They need to find a way to work the Ghostfacers into the story," Padalecki agrees. "I think there must be some place for them. Here's hoping."

The problem is that after seven seasons of *Supernatural*, there might actually be *too many* wonderful characters to fit into season 8. Continuing on from season 7, likely choices would seem to be Charlie, Garth, and the aforementioned Frank and Kevin. "We like all of those characters," says Singer. "And we'd certainly like to bring Meg and Sheriff Mills back. There are a bunch of people that we're fond of, really. Those characters give the show a continuum, so we're hoping to bring a number of people back."

ABOVE: Sam Winchester will find that the hunting life may not be for him anymore in season 8. OPPOSITE, TOP: Dean Winchester, however, will once again be reminded that hunting the supernatural is what he is really meant to do. OPPOSITE, BOTTOM: The boys both face uncertain and divergent futures after they are reunited in season 8.

SUPERNATURAL, THE MOVIE?

Despite the fans' wishes, *Supernatural* the television series will eventually end, but will that be the end? "I would do a *Supernatural* movie if we could do it right," creator Eric Kripke says. "I would do it if we could do it theatrically, if we could make it a true horror movie. I'd be very interested in that."

PREDICTING THE FUTURE

"The *Supernatural* fans are unbelievably passionate and supportive," points out co–executive producer Peter Johnson. "They've rallied around the show when it needed it, galvanized the audience to get the word out that it deserves to come back and come back and come back. The strength and passion of our fans is really unbelievable, and I think that is the number-one reason *Supernatural* keeps coming back. They are the people that show up and deliver us the ratings and get us back on The CW's schedule every year."

So for season 8, what new stories are there to tell, and what legends have yet to be explored? "There's a board of ideas that haven't been done yet, that are still fair game," says former executive producer Sera Gamble. For instance, co–executive producer Adam Glass reveals that one of the monsters on that board is a golem. "I just love the idea of a golem," he says. "People pitch it all the time. I know I've pitched it at least a couple times. I don't know if it'll ever get on the show, but I

love golems. I just think the idea is interesting. It's the Frankenstein's monster. It's the basis of the first monster. Really, I think you can argue that it's the foundation of every monster that's come since. Getting back to the beginning of monsters and doing something like that would be really cool."

Going even further back, consulting producer Ben Edlund suggests, "A dinosaur problem! That'd be interesting, but I don't know if that would ever happen." Executive producer Phil Sgriccia has a suggestion, too. "The Boggy Creek Monster! It's like a Yeti." Golems, dinosaurs, and abominable snowmen . . . how could they go wrong?

The rest of the ideas on the board have to remain a secret, of course, because you never know what will actually make its way into a *Supernatural* script. "I don't see an end to these stories," says executive story editor Robbie Thompson. "There's something so universal about them. *Supernatural* has such a rich world."

EPISODE GUIDE

SEASON 1

101: THE PILOT
Writer: Eric Kripke
Director: David Nutter
Locations: Lawrence, Kansas; Jericho, California

102: WENDIGO
Writers: Eric Kripke & Ron Milbauer & Terri Hughes Burton
Director: David Nutter
Location: Lost Creek, Colorado

103: DEAD IN THE WATER
Writers: Raelle Tucker & Sera Gamble
Director: Kim Manners
Location: Lake Manitoc, Wisconsin

104: PHANTOM TRAVELER
Writer: Richard Hatem
Director: Robert Singer
Locations: Lehigh Valley, Pennsylvania; Nazareth, Pennsylvania

105: BLOODY MARY
Writers: Terri Hughes Burton & Ron Milbauer
Director: Peter Ellis
Locations: Toledo, Ohio; Fort Wayne, Indiana

106: SKIN
Writer: John Shiban
Director: Robert Duncan McNeill
Location: St. Louis, Missouri

107: HOOK MAN
Writer: John Shiban
Director: David Jackson
Location: Ankeny, Iowa

108: BUGS
Writers: Rachel Nave & Bill Coakley
Director: Kim Manners
Locations: Oasis Plains, Oklahoma; Sapulpa, Oklahoma

109: HOME
Writer: Eric Kripke
Director: Ken Girotti
Location: Lawrence, Kansas

110: ASYLUM
Writer: Richard Hatem
Director: Guy Bee
Location: Rockford, Illinois

111: SCARECROW
Writer: John Shiban
Director: Kim Manners
Location: Burkitsville, Indiana

112: FAITH
Writers: Raelle Tucker & Sera Gamble
Director: Allan Kroeker
Location: Nebraska

113: ROUTE 666
Writers: Eugenie Ross-Leming & Brad Buckner
Director: Paul Shapiro
Location: Cape Girardeau, Mississippi

114: NIGHTMARE
Writers: Raelle Tucker & Sera Gamble
Director: Phil Sgriccia
Location: Saginaw, Michigan

115: THE BENDERS
Writer: John Shiban
Director: Peter Ellis
Location: Hibbing, Minnesota

116: SHADOW
Writer: Eric Kripke
Director: Kim Manners
Location: Chicago, Illinois

117: HELL HOUSE
Writer: Trey Callaway
Director: Chris Long
Location: Richardson, Texas

118: SOMETHING WICKED
Writer: Daniel Knauf
Director: Whitney Ransick
Locations: Fort Douglas, Wisconsin; Fitchburg, Wisconsin

119: PROVENANCE
Writer: David Ehrman
Director: Phil Sgriccia
Location: New Paltz, New York

120: DEAD MAN'S BLOOD
Writers: Cathryn Humphris & John Shiban
Director: Tony Wharmby
Location: Manning, Colorado

121: SALVATION
Writers: Raelle Tucker & Sera Gamble
Director: Robert Singer
Locations: Blue Earth, Minnesota; Manning, Colorado; Salvation, Iowa; Lincoln, Nebraska

122: DEVIL'S TRAP
Writer: Eric Kripke
Director: Kim Manners
Locations: Salvation, Iowa; Lincoln, Nebraska; Jefferson City, Missouri; Sioux Falls, South Dakota

OPPOSITE, TOP: A scene from episode 104, "Phantom Traveler." OPPOSITE, BOTTOM: The Winchesters investigate a ghost truck in episode 113, "Route 666."

SEASON 2

201: IN MY TIME OF DYING
Writer: Eric Kripke
Director: Kim Manners
Location: Sioux Falls, South Dakota

202: EVERYBODY LOVES A CLOWN
Writer: John Shiban
Director: Phil Sgriccia
Location: Medford, Wisconsin

203: BLOODLUST
Writer: Sera Gamble
Director: Robert Singer
Location: Red Lodge, Montana

204: CHILDREN SHOULDN'T PLAY WITH DEAD THINGS
Writer: Raelle Tucker
Director: Kim Manners
Location: Greenville, Illinois

205: SIMON SAID
Writer: Ben Edlund
Director: Tim Iacofano
Location: Guthrie, Oklahoma

206: NO EXIT
Writer: Matt Witten
Director: Kim Manners
Location: Philadelphia, Pennsylvania

207: THE USUAL SUSPECTS
Writer: Cathryn Humphris
Director: Mike Rohl
Location: Baltimore, Maryland

208: CROSSROAD BLUES
Writer: Sera Gamble
Director: Steve Boyum
Location: Greenwood, Mississippi

209: CROATOAN
Writer: John Shiban
Director: Robert Singer
Location: Rivergrove, Oregon

210: HUNTED
Writer: Raelle Tucker
Director: Rachel Talalay
Locations: Lafayette, Indiana; Peoria, Illinois

211: PLAYTHINGS
Writer: Matt Witten
Director: Charles Beeson
Location: Cornwall, Connecticut

212: NIGHTSHIFTER
Writer: Ben Edlund
Director: Phil Sgriccia
Location: Milwaukee, Wisconsin

213: HOUSES OF THE HOLY
Writer: Sera Gamble
Director: Kim Manners
Location: Providence, Rhode Island

214: BORN UNDER A BAD SIGN
Writer: Cathryn Humphris
Director: J. Miller Tobin
Locations: Twin Lakes, Wisconsin; Otter Creek, Iowa; Duluth, Minnesota; Sioux Falls, South Dakota

215: TALL TALES
Writer: John Shiban
Director: Bradford May
Location: Springfield, Ohio

216: ROADKILL
Writer: Raelle Tucker
Director: Charles Beeson
Location: Highway 41, Nevada

217: HEART
Writer: Sera Gamble
Director: Kim Manners
Location: San Francisco, California

218: HOLLYWOOD BABYLON
Writer: Ben Edlund
Director: Phil Sgriccia
Location: Los Angeles, California

219: FOLSOM PRISON BLUES
Writer: John Shiban
Director: Mike Rohl
Location: Little Rock, Arkansas

220: WHAT IS AND WHAT SHOULD NEVER BE
Writer: Raelle Tucker
Director: Eric Kripke
Location: Joliet, Illinois

221: ALL HELL BREAKS LOOSE, PART 1
Writer: Sera Gamble
Director: Bob Singer
Locations: Cold Oak, South Dakota; Sunrise, Wyoming

222: ALL HELL BREAKS LOOSE, PART 2
Story: Eric Kripke & Michael T. Moore
Teleplay: Eric Kripke
Director: Bob Singer
Locations: Cold Oak, South Dakota; Sunrise, Wyoming

SEASON 3

301: THE MAGNIFICENT SEVEN
Writer: Eric Kripke
Director: Kim Manners
Locations: Oak Park, Illinois; Lincoln, Nebraska

302: THE KIDS ARE ALRIGHT
Writer: Sera Gamble
Director: Phil Sgriccia
Location: Cicero, Indiana

303: BAD DAY AT BLACK ROCK
Writer: Ben Edlund
Director: Robert Singer
Locations: Buffalo, New York; Black Rock, New York; Queens, New York

304: SIN CITY
Writers: Robert Singer & Jeremy Carver
Director: Charles Beeson
Location: Elizabethville, Ohio

305: BEDTIME STORIES
Writer: Cathryn Humphris
Director: Mike Rohl
Location: Maple Springs, New York

306: RED SKY AT MORNING
Writer: Laurence Andries
Director: Cliff Bole
Location: Sea Pines, Massachusetts

307: FRESH BLOOD
Writer: Sera Gamble
Director: Kim Manners
Location: Albany, New York

OPPOSITE, TOP LEFT: The delightfully mulleted hunter Ash. OPPOSITE, TOP RIGHT: Jared Padalecki poses with iconic film star Linda Blair on the set of episode 207, "The Usual Suspects." OPPOSITE, BOTTOM: Dean dies again and again and again and again in episode 311, "Mystery Spot."

308: A VERY *SUPERNATURAL* CHRISTMAS
Writer: Jeremy Carver
Director: J. Michael Tobin
Locations: Ypsilanti, Michigan; Broken Bow, Nebraska

309: MALLEUS MALEFICARUM
Writer: Ben Edlund
Director: Robert Singer
Location: Sturbridge, Massachusetts

310: DREAM A LITTLE DREAM OF ME
Writers: Cathryn Humphris & Sera Gamble
Director: Steve Boyum
Location: Pittsburg, Pennsylvania

311: MYSTERY SPOT
Writers: Jeremy Carver & Emily McLaughlin
Director: Kim Manners
Location: Broward County, Florida

312: JUS IN BELLO
Writer: Sera Gamble
Director: Phil Sgriccia
Location: Monument, Colorado

313: GHOSTFACERS
Writer: Ben Edlund
Director: Phil Sgriccia
Location: Appleton, Wisconsin

314: LONG-DISTANCE CALL
Writer: Jeremy Carver
Director: Robert Singer
Location: Milan, Ohio

315: TIME IS ON MY SIDE
Writer: Sera Gamble
Director: Charles Beeson
Locations: Erie, Pennsylvania; Canaan, Vermont

316: NO REST FOR THE WICKED
Writer: Eric Kripke
Director: Kim Manners
Location: New Harmony, Indiana

SEASON 4

401: LAZARUS RISING
Writer: Eric Kripke
Director: Kim Manners
Location: Pontiac, Illinois

402: ARE YOU THERE, GOD? IT'S ME, DEAN WINCHESTER
Writer: Sera Gamble
Director: Phil Sgriccia
Location: Sioux Falls, South Dakota

403: IN THE BEGINNING
Writer: Jeremy Carver
Director: Steve Boyum
Locations: Sioux Falls, South Dakota; Lawrence, Kansas

404: METAMORPHOSIS
Writer: Cathryn Humphris
Director: Kim Manners
Location: Carthage, Missouri

405: MONSTER MOVIE
Writer: Ben Edlund
Director: Robert Singer
Location: Canonsburg, Pennsylvania

406: YELLOW FEVER
Writers: Andrew Dabb & Daniel Loflin
Director: Phil Sgriccia
Location: Rock Ridge, Colorado

407: IT'S THE GREAT PUMPKIN, SAM WINCHESTER
Writer: Julie Siege
Director: Charles Beeson

408: WISHFUL THINKING
Story: Ben Edlund & Lou Bollo
Teleplay: Ben Edlund
Director: Robert Singer
Location: Concrete, Washington

409: I KNOW WHAT YOU DID LAST SUMMER
Writer: Sera Gamble
Director: Charles Beeson

410: HEAVEN AND HELL
Story: Trevor Sands
Teleplay: Eric Kripke
Director: J. Miller Tobin
Location: Union, Kentucky

411: FAMILY REMAINS
Writer: Jeremy Carver
Director: Phil Sgriccia
Location: Stratton, Nebraska

412: CRISS ANGEL IS A DOUCHE BAG
Writer: Julie Siege
Director: Phil Sgriccia
Location: Sioux City, Iowa

413: AFTER SCHOOL SPECIAL
Writers: Andrew Dabb & Daniel Loflin
Director: Adam Kane
Location: Fairfax, Indiana

414: SEX AND VIOLENCE
Writer: Cathryn Humphris
Director: Charles Beeson
Location: Bedford, Iowa

415: DEATH TAKES A HOLIDAY
Writer: Jeremy Carver
Director: Steve Boyum
Location: Greybull, Wyoming

416: ON THE HEAD OF A PIN
Writer: Ben Edlund
Director: Mike Rohl
Location: Cheyenne, Wyoming

417: IT'S A TERRIBLE LIFE
Writer: Sera Gamble
Director: James Conway
Location: Ohio

418: THE MONSTER AT THE END OF THIS BOOK
Story: Julie Siege & Nancy Weiner
Teleplay: Julie Siege
Director: Mike Rohl
Location: Kripke's Hollow, Ohio

419: JUMP THE SHARK
Writers: Andrew Dabb & Daniel Loflin
Director: Phil Sgriccia
Location: Windom, Minnesota

420: THE RAPTURE
Writer: Jeremy Carver
Director: Charles Beeson
Location: Pontiac, Illinois

TOP: Ruby, Dean, and Sam prepare to face Alastair in episode 409, "I Know What You Did Last Summer." ABOVE: Castiel ponders his course of action in a scene from episode 416, "On the Head of a Pin."

TOP: Meg and a demon-possessed Bobby arrive with trouble in mind for Dean in episode 501, "Sympathy For the Devil." ABOVE: Dean sits down to a surprise dinner with Death in episode 521, "Two Minutes to Midnight." RIGHT: Sam and Dean take aim in a scene from episode 619, "Mommy Dearest."

421: WHEN THE LEVEE BREAKS
Writer: Sera Gamble
Director: Robert Singer
Locations: Sioux Falls, South Dakota; Jamestown, North Dakota; Elk River, Minnesota; Cold Spring, Minnesota

422: LUCIFER RISING
Writer: Eric Kripke
Director: Eric Kripke
Location: Ilchester, Maryland

SEASON 5

501: SYMPATHY FOR THE DEVIL
Writer: Eric Kripke
Director: Robert Singer
Locations: Ilchester, Maryland; Pike Creek, Delaware; Buffalo, New York

502: GOOD GOD, Y'ALL!
Writer: Sera Gamble
Director: Phil Sgriccia
Location: River Pass, Colorado

503: FREE TO BE YOU AND ME
Writer: Jeremy Carver
Director: J. Miller Tobin
Locations: Greeley, Pennsylvania; Garber, Oklahoma; Waterville, Maine

504: THE END
Writer: Ben Edlund
Director: Steve Boyum
Location: Kansas City, Missouri

505: FALLEN IDOLS
Writer: Julie Siege
Director: Jim Conway
Location: Canton, Ohio

506: I BELIEVE THE CHILDREN ARE OUR FUTURE
Writers: Andrew Dabb & Daniel Loflin
Director: Charles Beeson
Location: Alliance, Nebraska

507: THE CURIOUS CASE OF DEAN WINCHESTER
Story: Sera Gamble & Jenny Klein
Teleplay: Sera Gamble
Director: Robert Singer

508: CHANGING CHANNELS
Writer: Jeremy Carver
Director: Charles Beeson
Location: Wellington, Ohio

509: THE REAL GHOSTBUSTERS
Story: Nancy Weiner
Teleplay: Eric Kripke
Director: Jim Conway
Location: Vermillion, Ohio

510: ABANDON ALL HOPE
Writer: Ben Edlund
Director: Phil Sgriccia
Location: Carthage, Missouri

511: SAM, INTERRUPTED
Writers: Andrew Dabb & Daniel Loflin
Director: Jim Conway
Location: Ketchum, Oklahoma

512: SWAP MEAT
Story: Julie Siege & Rebecca Dessertine & Harvey Fedor
Teleplay: Julie Siege
Director: Robert Singer
Location: Housatonic, Massachusetts

513: THE SONG REMAINS THE SAME
Writers: Sera Gamble & Nancy Weiner
Director: Steve Boyum
Location: Lawrence, Kansas

514: MY BLOODY VALENTINE
Writer: Ben Edlund
Director: Mike Rohl
Location: Sioux Falls, South Dakota

515: DEAD MEN DON'T WEAR PLAID
Writer: Jeremy Carver
Director: John Showalter
Location: Sioux Falls, South Dakota

516: DARK SIDE OF THE MOON
Writers: Andrew Dabb & Daniel Loflin
Director: Jeff Woolnough
Location: Heaven

517: 99 PROBLEMS
Writer: Julie Siege
Director: Charles Beeson
Location: Blue Earth, Minnesota

518: POINT OF NO RETURN
Writer: Jeremy Carver
Director: Phil Sgriccia
Locations: Sioux Falls, South Dakota; Van Nuys, California

519: HAMMER OF THE GODS
Story: David Reed
Teleplay: Andrew Dabb & Daniel Loflin
Director: Rick Bota
Location: Muncie, Indiana

520: THE DEVIL YOU KNOW
Writer: Ben Edlund
Director: Robert Singer
Location: West Nevada

521: TWO MINUTES TO MIDNIGHT
Writer: Sera Gamble
Director: Phil Sgriccia
Locations: Davenport, Iowa; Chicago, Illinois

522: SWAN SONG
Story: Eric "Giz" Gewirtz
Teleplay: Eric Kripke
Director: Steve Boyum
Locations: Detroit, Michigan; Lawrence, Kansas

SEASON 6

601: EXILE ON MAIN STREET
Writer: Sera Gamble
Director: Phil Sgriccia
Location: Cicero, Indiana

602: TWO AND A HALF MEN
Writer: Adam Glass
Director: John Showalter
Location: Lansing, Michigan

603: THE THIRD MAN
Writer: Ben Edlund
Director: Robert Singer
Location: Easter, Pennsylvania

604: WEEKEND AT BOBBY'S
Writers: Andrew Dabb & Daniel Loflin
Director: Jensen Ackles
Locations: Sioux Falls, South Dakota; Kenosha, Wisconsin

605: LIVE FREE OR TWI-HARD
Writer: Brett Matthews
Director: Rod Hardy
Location: Limestone, Illinois

606: YOU CAN'T HANDLE THE TRUTH
Story: David Reed & Eric Charmelo &
Nicole Snyder
Teleplay: Eric Charmelo &
Nicole Snyder
Director: Jan Eliasberg
Location: Calumet City, Illinois

607: FAMILY MATTERS
Writers: Andrew Dabb & Daniel Loflin
Director: Guy Bee
Location: Lansing, Michigan

608: ALL DOGS GO TO HEAVEN
Writer: Adam Glass
Director: Phil Sgriccia
Location: Buffalo, New York

**609: CLAP YOUR HANDS IF
YOU BELIEVE**
Writer: Ben Edlund
Director: John Showalter
Location: Elwood, Indiana

610: CAGED HEAT
Story: Jenny Klein & Brett Matthews
Teleplay: Brett Matthews
Director: Robert Singer
Location: Evergreen, Montana

611: APPOINTMENT IN SAMARRA
Writers: Sera Gamble & Robert Singer
Director: Mike Rohl
Location: Sioux Falls, South Dakota

612: LIKE A VIRGIN
Writer: Adam Glass
Director: Phil Sgriccia
Location: Portland, Oregon

613: UNFORGIVEN
Writers: Andrew Dabb & Daniel Loflin
Director: David Barrett
Location: Bristol, Rhode Island

614: MANNEQUIN 3: THE RECKONING
Writers: Eric Charmelo &
Nicole Snyder
Director: Jeannot Szwarc
Location: Paterson, New Jersey

615: THE FRENCH MISTAKE
Writer: Ben Edlund
Director: Charles Beeson
Location: Vancouver, British Columbia,
Canada

616: . . . AND THEN THERE WERE NONE
Writer: Brett Matthews
Director: Mike Rohl
Location: Sandusky, Ohio

617: MY HEART WILL GO ON
Writers: Eric Charmelo &
Nicole Snyder
Director: Phil Sgriccia
Locations: Sioux Falls, South Dakota;
Chester, Pennsylvania

618: FRONTIERLAND
Story: Jackson Stewart &
Andrew Dabb & Daniel Loflin
Teleplay: Andrew Dabb &
Daniel Loflin
Director: Guy Bee
Location: Sunrise, Wyoming

619: MOMMY DEAREST
Writer: Adam Glass
Director: John Showalter
Location: Grants Pass, Oregon

620: THE MAN WHO WOULD BE KING
Writer: Ben Edlund
Director: Ben Edlund
Locations: Bootbock, Kansas;
Sioux Falls, South Dakota

621: LET IT BLEED
Writer: Sera Gamble
Director: John Showalter
Locations: Bootbock, Kansas;
Sioux Falls, South Dakota

622: THE MAN WHO KNEW TOO MUCH
Writer: Eric Kripke
Director: Robert Singer
Locations: Bootbock, Kansas;
Sioux Falls, South Dakota

SEASON 7

701: MEET THE NEW BOSS
Writer: Sera Gamble
Director: Phil Sgriccia
Locations: Bootbock, Kansas;
Sioux Falls, South Dakota

702: HELLO, CRUEL WORLD
Writer: Ben Edlund
Director: Guy Bee
Locations: Bootbock, Kansas; Stockville,
Kansas; Sioux Falls, South Dakota

703: THE GIRL NEXT DOOR
Writers: Andrew Dabb & Daniel Loflin
Director: Jensen Ackles
Location: Bozeman, Montana

704: DEFENDING YOUR LIFE
Writer: Adam Glass
Director: Robert Singer
Location: Dearborn, Michigan

705: SHUT UP, DR. PHIL
Writers: Brad Buckner &
Eugenie Ross-Leming
Director: Phil Sgriccia
Location: Prosperity, Indiana

706: SLASH FICTION
Writer: Robbie Thompson
Director: John Showalter
Locations: Whitefish, Montana;
Ankeny, Iowa

707: THE MENTALISTS
Writers: Ben Acker & Ben Blacker
Director: Mike Rohl
Location: Lily Dale, New York

**708: SEASON 7, TIME FOR A
WEDDING!**
Writers: Andrew Dabb & Daniel Loflin
Director: Tim Andrew
Location: Pike Creek, Delaware

**709: HOW TO WIN FRIENDS AND
INFLUENCE MONSTERS**
Writer: Ben Edlund
Director: Guy Bee
Location: Hammonton, New Jersey

710: DEATH'S DOOR
Writer: Sera Gamble
Director: Robert Singer
Location: Hammonton, New Jersey

711: ADVENTURES IN BABYSITTING
Writer: Adam Glass
Director: Jeannot Szwarc
Location: Dodge City, Kansas

ABOVE: *Jim Beaver, Jared Padalecki, and Jensen Ackles pose for the cameras.*

712: TIME AFTER TIME
Writer: Robbie Thompson
Director: Phil Sgriccia
Location: Canton, Ohio

713: THE SLICE GIRLS
Writers: Eugenie Ross-Leming &
Brad Buckner
Director: Jerry Wanek
Location: Seattle, Washington

**714: PLUCKY PENNYWHISTLE'S
MAGICAL MENAGERIE**
Writers: Andrew Dabb & Daniel Loflin
Director: Mike Rohl
Location: Wichita, Kansas

715: REPO MAN
Writer: Ben Edlund
Director: Thomas J. Wright
Location: Coeur d'Alene, Idaho

716: OUT WITH THE OLD
Writers: Robert Singer & Jenny Klein
Director: John F. Showalter
Location: Portland, Oregon

717: THE BORN-AGAIN IDENTITY
Writer: Sera Gamble
Director: Robert Singer
Location: Northern Indiana

718: PARTY ON, GARTH
Writer: Adam Glass
Director: Phil Sgriccia
Location: Junction City, Kansas

719: OF GRAVE IMPORTANCE
Writers: Eugenie Ross-Leming &
Brad Buckner
Director: Tim Andrew
Location: Bodega Bay, California

**720: THE GIRL WITH THE DUNGEONS
AND DRAGONS TATTOO**
Writer: Robbie Thompson
Director: John MacCarthy
Location: Chicago, Illinois

721: READING IS FUNDAMENTAL
Writer: Ben Edlund
Director: Ben Edlund
Location: Neighbor, Michigan

722: THERE WILL BE BLOOD
Writers: Andrew Dabb & Daniel Loflin
Director: Guy Bee
Location: Hoople, North Dakota

723: SURVIVAL OF THE FITTEST
Writer: Sera Gamble
Director: Robert Singer
Location: Bozeman, Montana

Jared Padalecki

Jensen Ackles

ACKNOWLEDGMENTS

In Vancouver, BC: Jerry Wanek, John Marcynuk, Mary-Ann Liu, Lee-Anne Elaschuk, Robert Leader, Andrei Adrianko, Suzi Levoguer, Chris Cooper, Ivan Hayden, Toby Lindala, George Neuman, Dawn Grey

In LA: Eric Kripke, Rebecca Dessertine, David Reed, and Jackson Stewart

At Warner Bros.: Holly Ollis, Carol Marks-George, Diana Pearson, Thane Christopher, Marc Klein, Anna Songco, JoAnne Narcisse, and Sheffia Lenox

The author would also like to thank: Christopher Cerasi, Tara Larsen, Jim Michaels, everyone who graciously shared their valuable time for interviews, everyone at Insight Editions, and his family, with special thanks to his wife, Thya

COLOPHON

Publisher: Raoul Goff
Art Director: Chrissy Kwasnik
Designer: *tabula rasa* graphic design
Acquiring Editor: Robbie Schmidt
Editor: Chris Prince
Project Manager: Christopher Cerasi
Associate Managing Editor: Jan Hughes
Production Manager: Anna Wan

Insight Editions would like to thank Amy Wideman, Binh Matthews, Mark Nichol, Spencer Stucky, Shira Engel, and Leigh Stewart.

PHOTO CREDITS

All images courtesy of Warner Bros.